General editor: Graham Handley MA PhD

Brodie's Notes on Jane Austen's

Persuasion

Kevin Dowling MA
Head of English Department, Bembridge School

Pan Books London and Sydney

First published 1986 by Pan Books Ltd
Cavaye Place, London SW10 9PG
9 8 7 6 5 4 3 2 1
© Pan Books Ltd 1986
ISBN 0 330 50221 2
Photoset by Parker Typesetting Service, Leicester
Printed and bound in Great Britain by
Richard Clay (The Chaucer Press) Ltd, Bungay, Suffolk

Contents

Page references in these Notes are to the
Pan Classics edition of *Persuasion*
but as references are also given to
particular chapters, the Notes my be
used with any edition of the book.

throughout → d'1 bout à l'autre
plot → intrigue

Preface

The intention throughout this study aid is to stimulate and guide, to encourage the reader's *involvement* in the text, to develop disciplined critical responses and a sure understanding of the main details in the chosen text.

Brodie's Notes provide a summary of the plot of the play or novel followed by act, scene or chapter summaries, each of which will have an accompanying critical commentary designed to underline the most important literary and factual details. Textual notes will be explanatory or critical (sometimes both), defining what is difficult or obscure on the one hand, or stressing points of character, style or plot on the other. Revision questions will be set on each act or group of chapters to test the student's careful application to the text of the prescribed book.

The second section of each of these study aids will consist of a critical examination of the author's art. This will cover such major elements as characterization, style, structure, setting, theme(s) or any other aspect of the book which the editor considers needs close study. The paramount aim is to send the student back to the text. Each study aid will include a series of general questions which require a detailed knowledge of the set book; the first of these questions will have notes by the editor of what *might* be included in a written answer. A short list of books considered useful as background reading for the student will be provided at the end.

Graham Handley

Literary terms used in these notes

antithesis The balancing of two opposing ideas or contrasting expressions, often within a sentence. The purpose is to heighten the effect of what is said.

epigram A witticism, sharp and concise, sometimes involving an apparent contradiction.

implied reader The novelist is telling the story, consciously or unconsciously, to an imagined reader who shares her judgement of character and conduct, her outlook on life.

irony A deeper meaning derived from the opposite of what is stated literally. The Greek origin of the word is *eironeia*, pretended ignorance.

narrative voice The narration is by an authoritative, all-knowing (omniscient) narrator. Sometimes this 'voice' will assume a particular tone (e.g. sympathetic, sarcastic, reflective), or assume the verbal or mental nuances of a particular character.

naturalism Truth to Nature. Detailed presentation of scene.

paradox An apparent contradiction which is true nevertheless.

realism convincing, life-like portrayal of character, and representation of conduct and thought.

rhetorical Persuasive, in an oratorical style; having the structure and flavour of a formal speech.

satire Mocking, e.g. pretension and self-deception, this form of wit often exaggerates or distorts a surface reality to emphasize the underlying truth.

Jane Austen and the Novel

Anyone taking up *Persuasion* is quickly aware of the importance Jane Austen attached to reading. She herself enjoyed particularly the novels of Richardson, the poetry of Crabbe and Cowper and the prose of her 'dear' Dr Johnson. Her writing, however, owes little to her predecessors or contemporaries. The famous comments, from her letters, that 'three or four families in a country village' was the thing to work on, on a 'little bit (two inches wide) of ivory' were not intended for publication and tell us little. This most retiring of authors insisted that her books were written 'by a lady' or 'by the author of *Pride and Prejudice, Mansfield Park* etc.', refused the temptations of the literary world, and was embarrassed by the patronage of the Prince Regent. She became a writer from 'taste and inclination' (Henry Austen's biographical note), 'for her own amusement' (J. E. Austen-Leigh's *Memoir*). That she was a conscious artist is clear from her letters, and the constant re-working and revising of her material. The fact remains, however, that she wrote practically nothing about her art.

'Human nature in the midland counties' is much the same as it is anywhere else, and Chawton was as happy a place as any from which to watch the world go by – the post-chaises full of 'future heroes, legislators, fools and villains'. What gives a unique pleasure is the combination of sharply drawn characters, control and elegance of style, the intricate structure of the novels, and their pervasive irony. They do give us 'the most thorough knowledge of human nature, the happiest delineation of its varieties, the liveliest effusions of wit and humour … conveyed to the world in the best chosen language' (*Northanger Abbey*).

The scale of Jane Austen's novels is not grand. The restriction of locality and circumstance is a deliberate limitation of material. She was indeed writing within the conventions of the day, mainly about one class, of young women – and young men, as they were seen by women, of relationships leading to marriage. This sometimes gives rise to the supposition that 'Aunt Jane' described the gyrations of marionettes in 'elegant but confined houses' (Charlotte Brontë) and their gentlemen who occasion-

to take up → aborder
to owe →
inches → pouce (2,54 cm)
ivory → ivoire
intended for → fiancé
retiring →

ally went to London 'on 'orseback for 'air-cuts and shaves' (*The Janeites*, Rudyard Kipling), presumably because 'of events her life was singularly barren: few changes and no great crisis ever broke this smooth current of its course' (*A Memoir of Jane Austen* J.E. Austen-Leigh 1870).

An intelligent, vivacious woman from a large, loving family in the south of England at the end of the eighteenth century, Jane Austen did not live in seclusion from the ordinary – and still less from the extraordinary – in contemporary life. Two of her brothers served with great distinction in Nelson's navy; her cousin's husband was guillotined; her aunt was falsely accused of theft and had been in danger of being transported; her brother Henry ('his mind is not a mind for affliction', Jane said) was a soldier, a banker, then a clergyman; another brother, Edward, was adopted by a very wealthy, distant relative and was eventually made his heir, and was thus able to give Jane, Cassandra and their mother a home at Chawton. In a sense, therefore, she chose to write about less than she knew: the novels are not melodramatic; no one dies; children scarcely exist; servants are not seen or heard; there is no lasting sorrow. On the periphery, it is true, one can glimpse the shadows of bankruptcy, poverty, illegitimacy, adultery and illness, but the interest is in character primarily, and not in circumstance. If guilt and misery are there, the comic spirit does not dwell on them, and there is neither tragedy nor poetry to give this particular imagined world a closer resemblance to the real.

In some ways Jane Austen's work looks to the 19th- and 20th-century novel. Her novels are studies in the way the world is perceived, the way the mind works. The problem of learning to recognize the truth is seen as one of necessary self-discovery, a maturing of character through adversity. The individual and his convictions are seen within society and its codes. Language is a refractory medium, giving expression to the inexpressibly personal from within a conventional structure. The sympathy with romanticism is not an allegiance, however. The daughter of a gentleman and a clergyman, Jane Austen accepted the world and her place in it. Her realism is predominantly an examination of the rational, exterior evidence, from a static view of character. She regards change and decay drily, with ambivalence. Conflict of principle is resolved ideally. There is the finality of belief in Providence. The antithetical structure of her novels (pride and prejudice, sense and sensibility, Mansfield Park as it is and as it ought to be, Northanger Gothic and Bath smoking in the rain, Emma before and after understanding, persuasion or principle) assumes the possibility and necessity of balance, of a resolution achieved by the protagonist aligning herself with what is absolute.

match → mariage
lavish → prodiguer
unwilling → décidé
at length → enfin
removal → déménage:
ground → terrain
to serve → servir

match → mariage
lavish → prodiguer
unwilling → décidé
at length → enfin
removal → déménage:
ground → terrain

p. 11 et 12

Plot summary

Persuasion is the story of Anne Elliot, the second daughter of Sir Walter Elliot of Kellynch Hall in Somerset. Seven years before the story opens, Anne had fallen in love with Captain Frederick Wentworth, an intelligent but poor naval officer, and had become engaged to him. Her father had disapproved of the match but when Anne's great friend and adviser, Lady Russell, also spoke strongly against it, Anne broke the engagement, whereupon her lover left the country.

When the novel begins, Sir Walter, who is a vain and stupid man, finds himself so heavily in debt that he must learn to live on a less lavish scale. He is very unwilling to let Kellynch Hall, but is eventually persuaded by his agent, Mr Shepherd, and Lady Russell, that Admiral and Mrs Croft would make desirable tenants. At length the business is arranged, and just before the removal takes place, Anne discovers, to her embarrassment, that Mrs Croft is the sister of Captain Wentworth.

Sir Walter and his eldest daughter, Elizabeth, who is as proud and as vain as her father, now set out for Bath, accompanied by Mrs Clay, the widowed daughter of Mr Shepherd, while Anne goes to visit Mary, her married sister. Mary, her husband Charles Musgrove and two sons live at Uppercross Cottage in the grounds of the Great House where her husband's family dwell. It is not long before Admiral and Mrs Croft begin to pay calls in the neighbourhood and, naturally, they come to the Great House. Mrs Croft talks of her brother who, Mrs Musgrove discovers, was once in command of a ship on which her scapegrace son, Dick Musgrove, now dead, had served. Anne dreads meeting Captain Wentworth, and for a while succeeds in avoiding him. At last, however, he comes to the Cottage and she sees him again. The situation is not as awkward as she had imagined it would be, and she accepts it calmly. Mary's two sisters-in-law, Henrietta and Louisa are much in the company of Captain Wentworth and Anne imagines he is in love with one of them. During a morning walk in the autumn, however, she realizes that Henrietta is in love with her cousin, Charles Hayter, of whom the snobbish Mary disapproves.

Captain Wentworth now pays a visit to a friend at Lyme Regis, and when the Musgrove girls hear of this, they, too, plan an excursion. Several important events occur during this excursion. First, they meet a Captain Benwick; secondly, they see Mr Elliot, a distant cousin and Sir Walter's heir; and thirdly, Louisa falls on the Cobb and is seriously hurt. For a while Anne is involved in the misfortunes of the family at Uppercross, but she soon departs for Bath to live with her father and sister. Here she finds herself in a different and less congenial world. Sir Walter has taken a house where he and Elizabeth entertain the society of the city. Mrs Clay is still with them, acting as companion to Elizabeth, but Anne fears that she may be hoping to persuade Sir Walter to marry her. Mr Elliot who has been recently widowed, is a frequent visitor to the house. He has had no connections with Sir Walter and his family for many years but is now anxious to renew his acquaintance with his cousins, and, if possible, to prevent Sir Walter from marrying again. Anne is at first pleased to see him and thinks he will marry Elizabeth, but it is soon obvious that it is Anne whom he admires. Meanwhile she learns, to her surprise, that Captain Benwick and Louisa Musgrove have fallen in love and become engaged.

Not long after this announcement, Anne meets Captain Wentworth on several occasions and begins to hope that he may still be in love with her. She also realizes Mr Elliott's intentions towards herself, partly through an old schoolfellow, Mrs Smith, who has known Mr Elliot in his younger days. Presently Anne's sister Mary arrives in Bath accompanied by most of the Musgrove family. Henrietta Musgrove is to marry her cousin, Charles Hayter, and has come to Bath to buy her trousseau. Anne now knows that she has nothing to fear from either of the Musgrove girls, and soon after, when she is visiting Mrs Musgrove at her hotel, Captain Wentworth gives her a letter in which he declares that he has always loved her. The story ends with the marriage of Anne and Captain Wentworth, the altered circumstances of the Captain having persuaded Sir Walter and Lady Russell to change their minds.

Chapter summaries, critical commentaries, textual notes and revision questions

Chapter 1

In the summer of 1814, Sir Walter Elliot, baronet, a widower with one married daughter, and two living with him at Kellynch Hall, is finding that his family estate does not provide an income to cover the expenses of his household.

Commentary

Sir Walter's embarrassments are of his own making. Without the responsible guidance of Lady Elliot the baronet lives beyond his means, encouraged by his eldest daughter who shares her father's ideas of what is due to rank and beauty. The estate is entailed and cannot be mortgaged further; Sir Walter having no son, the heir presumptive is the William Walter Eliott whom Elizabeth had 'meant' to marry.

The author's detached, ironic tone of narration offers an absurdly literal statement of Sir Walter's view of himself. The 'book of books' is the only literature the baronet chooses to read and his interest is always aroused by the entry made in his own name. His family's history is handsomely reduced to two duodecimo pages of printer's work. The empty-headed narcissism of Sir Walter is established before the formal, literal, omniscient narrative voice outlines his history and character. By the balanced intricacy of prose that gives a wonderful portrait of nothing, the reader feels the preposterous vanity before a statement of it is made; and there is an implied contrast between the values of Elliot of Kellynch Hall and those shared by the author, the reader, and people of 'real understanding'. Preoccupation with personal appearance and social standing is ridiculed by belittling comparison with the 'real' respectability that recognizes the qualities of Anne and the 'right-mindedness' of her mother. There is an appeal to a notion of reality unknown to Sir Walter and Elizabeth. Anne, by contrast, generous and intelligent, is alone in a family by whose measurement she is 'nobody'. Elizabeth's predicament may be unenviable, but the critical tone of the account of her mercenary selfishness makes it impossible for us to sympathize with her regrets and apprehensions as she approaches the 'years of danger'. Through the concentration on the spurious looking-glass world of the Elliots, and the mentioning of Anne for the most part in an ironic affectation of Sir Walter's view of her as a 'faded and thin' creature of 'inferior value', self-deception is seen as oppressive; the disregarded dependence of Anne's position is the more poignant for its understatement.

Baronetage *Debrett's Peerage, Baronetage, Knightage, and Companionage,* first published in 1802, listing the members of the family of each baronet together with a brief account of the family's history.

Limited remnant of the earliest patents . . . endless creations Sir Walter respects ancient holders of titles and scorns those families which have acquired nobility relatively recently.

Dugdale Compiled *The Baronage of England* in the seventeenth century.

awful legacy i.e. the legacy would have filled a responsible father with awe.

unreasonable applications i.e. Sir Walter's attempts at re-marriage have been rebuffed; by inference, the ladies were wealthier and/or of a higher station than the baronet.

chaise and four A carriage pulled by four horses.

after Lady Elliot's death The entail of the estate requires male succession. Sir Walter, a widower without a son, now sees the heir presumptive as a future son-in-law.

Tattersal's A club for the racing fraternity; a place for the fashionable to be seen (like the lobby of the House of Commons).

black ribbons Elizabeth is nominally in mourning for her cousin's wife.

alienable Able to be sold off separately.

Chapter 2

Mr Shepherd, Sir Walter's agent, and Lady Russell – supported by Anne – advise radical economies which Sir Walter and Elizabeth cannot countenance. Instead, Kellynch Hall is to be let and the family will live at Bath.

Commentary

The chapter is a pattern of persuasion; honesty, justice, respectability, prudence, true dignity and principle fail to make an impression on self-importance and the feelings of a gentleman. Mr Shepherd, shrewdly practical and self-interested, leaves

Lady Russell to propose a course of action unavoidable but unpopular. He takes advantage of Sir Walter's recoil from the disgrace of living without ostentation to propose the evacuation of Kellynch in favour of the potentially less expensive Bath.

Lady Russell's efforts are earnest and disinterested, although her prejudices on the side of 'rank and consequence' and a fondness for Bath make her overlook Anne's wishes in what are defined as Anne's best interests.

Anne's opinions are derided; her vigorous and rigid recommendations are unpalatable even when tentatively voiced by Lady Russell. Bath is a further humiliation, a reverse that is typical of Anne's fate. The debate is sketched in such a way as to dramatize Anne's relative unimportance. The introduction of Mrs Clay, Mr Shepherd's daughter, as the clever, artful confidante of Elizabeth serves to emphasize the dwindling significance of her sister. 'Injustice' and 'discredit' triumph.

have the *disagreeable* prompted Mr Shepherd would rather Lady Russell made the unwelcome recommendations.
only a knight Below a baronet; a title which cannot be inherited.
knocked off Dispensed with. Note the 'comforts' and 'decencies' listed.
London, Bath or . . . London is most attractive, but expensive. Bath is fashionable and less costly.
unexceptionable i.e. an applicant who was acceptable to the exacting Sir Walter.
friendship quite out of place i.e. their different positions in a well-defined class structure and their association unlikely and, to Lady Russell, unseemly.

Chapter 3

Mr Shepherd suggests that a naval officer, wealthy from the war, might make an ideal tenant. Admiral Croft expresses interest in becoming the tenant of Kellynch Hall, and is accepted.

Commentary

The conversation is reported without descriptive embellishment. What comment is implicit in the narrative is more telling for its relative scarcity ('she stopt a moment to consider what might do for the clergyman' – 'expressed as strong an inclination for the place as a man who knew it only by description, could feel').

Mr Shepherd, calculated and efficient in his rehearsed spontaneity, contrives the acceptance in principle of a naval officer. The assiduous flattery ('consequence has its tax') prepares the baronet to accept the unpalatable as tribute. Sir Walter sees himself as conferring a favour in condescending to take the Admiral as a tenant. It is partly in order to excuse himself from the demeaning necessity of commerce that Sir Walter speaks patronizingly of the 'profession' and its 'utility'. His objection to the service is that it brings 'undue distinction' upon those who have earned and not inherited it; and that its hard, physical demands weather a man beyond what is decorous in polite society. Sir Walter's speeches, preposterous in their vanity and insensitivity, are an indictment of snobbery.

Anne speaks for the first time; her brief, rational defence of the navy is quietly moving. It is stifled by her father who finds it natural to disregard anyone unconnected with property. Mr Shepherd is 'eloquent' in his persuasion of Sir Walter; Anne's still small voice is inaudible. Ironically, it is Anne who is most attentive to the decision in which she has played no part.

peace . . . rich navy officers ashore The peace is that of 1814, the end of the Napoleonic wars. 'Prize' money was received from the government as reward for captured enemy ships. Sir Walter describes Kellynch as 'a prize indeed'.

consequence has its tax i.e. the privilege of importance and rank in the community naturally brings with it the interest and curiosity of inferiors.

not . . . disposed to favour a tenant i.e. Sir Walter parades his intention of resisting the rights of any tenant.

persons of obscure birth into distinction The navy was the service in which merit alone could earn promotion; wealth and patronage were less important than in any other profession.

powder The Admiral is bald.

Chapter 4

The brother-in-law of Admiral Croft of whom Anne Elliot was thinking is revealed as Captain Frederick Wentworth. Almost eight years earlier he and Anne had been deeply in love and intended to marry. Anne was persuaded by Lady Russell that, given the uncertainty of the young man's prospects, the engagement was unwise. Now that Admiral Croft is to be the tenant of Kellynch Hall, Anne is agitated at the probability of again meeting Captain Wentworth.

Commentary

In a sense this is the core of the novel. The retrospect is a statement of several views of the possible marriage between Anne Elliot and Captain Wentworth, an examination of the manner of their separation and a weighing of the consequences; most important is Anne's own assessment of her behaviour. The narrative is a classic illustration of Jane Austen's formal style (paragraph 3 is an interesting exception) – balanced, elegant, precisely informative, with no immediate drama or conversation, little shift of the narrative point of view from detached omniscience, and fewer touches than usual of her characteristic irony.

Anne's life now, blighted as it appears to be by the past, is the subject of the story. The intensity of feeling and complexity of reasoning over the past are presented here as the unresolved matter of the present. The manner and tone of narration are governed by this intention.

Captain Wentworth's claims as a suitor are directly stated, as are Anne's attractive qualities. The romance is ideal, but the blunt realism of 'Half the sum of attraction, on either side, might have been enough, for he had nothing to do, and she had hardly any body to love' preserves us from sentimentality. Captain Wentworth had no income other than his professional pay; he had to make his way. The 'steadiness of opinion and tenderness of nature' of Lady Russell, surrogate mother as she is, had persuaded Anne to believe that she should not engage herself indefinitely. Ironies abound; it was 'principally for the advantage of the young man that Anne had come to see the match as imprudent'; she is blamed by Captain Wentworth for what seems to him to be weakness; the Captain is successful, prosperous and free, whereas Anne languishes confined. In the narration there is a wistful sadness over wasted lives, and a ruthless recognition of the inevitability of the admittedly 'unnatural' adoption of the prudent course. Lady Russell had acted from the best of motives and although Anne now believes the advice to have been wrong in itself and not merely in its incorrect forecast, she does not blame Lady Russell's intention or her own acquiescence. To Anne, and Jane Austen, the conflict of duty and inclination could not have been resolved in any other way.

doing nothing i.e. refusing to provide her with any fortune or income.
station A port or naval base, with the chance of action, promotion and
  prizes.
left the country i.e. left that part of the country.
navy lists Published details of postings.
a single man at the time Unmarried and therefore presumably less
  likely to confide to anyone the story of his brother's broken
  engagement.

Chapter 5

Admiral and Mrs Croft have seen Kellynch Hall and like it. Sir
Walter approves of them, and arrangements are made for let-
ting the house and grounds. Elizabeth and her father, accompanied by Mrs Clay, leave for Bath. Anne's younger sister, Mary,
asks for her company and help at Uppercross Cottage. Mary and
Anne call on the Musgroves and their daughters, Henrietta and
Louisa, at the Great House.

Commentary

In stating Anne's ambivalent attitude to the arrival of the Crofts,
the first sentence is a lightly ironic preface to a narrative that
now focuses on the immediate present, and in which Anne's
emotions, perceptiveness, judgements and patience are central.

Anne recognizes that Mrs Clay, young and personable as she
is, despite evident imperfections by the exacting standards of Sir
Walter and Elizabeth, may well succeed in persuading Sir Walter
that he might wish to marry again. The warning, given to Elizabeth out of a sense of duty rather than from a wish to interfere,
is rebuffed. Anne's being claimed by Mary because she is useful
at Uppercross and unwanted in Bath, is another 'affront' in its
casual disregard, but nevertheless is realistically accepted as
having at least the consolation of purpose.

Mary Musgrove, introduced as being thoughtlessly selfish, is
quickly established as a petulant hypochondriac. Without
'resources for solitude' she is prey to the vicissitudes of family
life – which is not at all what any young lady who lives to be
'fashionable, happy and merry' has a right to expect. As Mary
complains of her children, her husband and her relations, the
effect is to stress the narrowness of Anne's life and the absence
of possibilities for fulfilment.

The subject matter is mundane to the point of triviality, the tone satirically revealing. As always the standpoint for judgement is Anne herself. Mary lacks fortitude. Elizabeth's vanity may appear to protect her from unwelcome reality, but it is a weakness. The Musgrove girls have the 'usual stock of accomplishments', are pleasant and affectionate, but are less intelligent and cultured than Anne. Society such as this seems to emphasize Anne's isolation.

'This indenture sheweth' The tenancy agreement would begin with the required legal flourish.

never set the Thames on fire Never do anything remarkable.

Elizabeth . . . more to be pitied than herself If Sir Walter were to marry Mrs Clay, Elizabeth would no longer be mistress of Kellynch Hall. If there were to be an heir, then most of her inheritance would also be lost.

nice See p.21.

you will not like to call . . . have been to see you? Mary is conscious of her social position. The Musgroves, untitled landowners, 'ought' to pay the first call on a baronet's daughter.

Revision questions on Chapters 1–5

1 What do we learn about the characters of Elizabeth and Mary?

2 What is Sir Walter's opinion of naval officers, and how was he persuaded to let Kellynch Hall to Admiral Croft?

3 What do we learn of the love of Anne Elliot and Captain Wentworth eight years earlier?

4 What do we learn of Lady Russell?

5 Write an essay on Jane Austen's use of irony in these chapters.

Chapter 6

The support and confidante of all, Anne makes the best of her stay at Uppercross. The Crofts arrive at Kellynch; they visit the Great House at Uppercross, bringing news of the imminent arrival of Mrs Croft's brother. Mrs Musgrove remembers the name Wentworth as that of a former captain of her dead son, Richard, and the family look forward to meeting the officer.

Commentary

Anne is the intermediary between her sister and the Musgrove family. Principally, Mary objects to their casual disregard for the formalities of social relationships; and the Musgroves find Mary's insistence on 'place' tiresome and ungracious. Charles is an earnest sportsman, tolerant of his wife's 'unreasonableness', who confides in Anne but not (in view of the past, see p.42) in any personal or intense way. Once again, slight as the matter may seem, it establishes Anne as the one person who is trusted and depended upon by everyone. The activity is 'wholesome' – a distraction. This centrality, however, brings with it the poignancy of exclusion as, although Anne is in demand because of her personal qualities, she remains curiously invisible and unwanted for herself. Mr and Mrs Musgrove inquire about Sir Walter's settling in Bath, but do not wait for an answer; Anne's playing is useful and gives her pleasure, but is not listened to.

The tone is occasionally sharply sardonic. The Musgroves, harmless and kindly, 'had their own game to guard and to destroy'; Mary and her husband 'might pass for a happy couple', and 'poor Richard' is really 'thick-headed, unfeeling, unprofitable Dick'. The delicate helplessness of an intelligent, dependent woman, suffering an emotional trial alone, unable to ask questions she fears to have answered, is described literally (see final paragraph p.56) and commented upon obliquely by ironic observation of well-intentioned obtuseness.

Mrs Charles Note the abbreviated formality. Anne is 'Miss Anne' to Mrs Musgrove, who is of lower rank. Mary is Mrs Charles Musgrove.

there being no means of her going Charles can transport only himself and his wife.

she could now answer as she ought Anne had not known what to say in answer to Mrs Croft's earlier remark. Ironically, she misinterprets the information that 'he' is married.

paid off On half-pay until required again for action.

Chapter 7

Captain Wentworth arrives at Kellynch. Mr Musgrove calls on him there and invites him to Uppercross. Mary's eldest son is injured in a fall and Anne offers to remain with the child while Mary and Charles dine at the Great House and are introduced to Captain Wentworth. This visit is returned the next day, and Anne and Captain Wentworth meet briefly.

Commentary

The domestic upset of a child's accident postpones the inevitable meeting with Captain Wentworth – still referred to formally, as Anne must think of him. Despite her evident anxiety for her nephew, and the diversion of activity necesssary after the accident, Anne is conscious of this escape. Anne's management of affairs, unassuming, confident and efficient, leads naturally to Charles's convenient declaration that this is a 'female case' and that there is nothing in it to require a father to shut himself up, and even less acceptably to Mary's striking assertion that Anne, who 'has not a mother's feelings', ought to be the one to stay with the invalid. The conversations are sometimes reported freely in a telescoped style for brevity and the effect of the movement of thought of the individual (see p.62, paragraph 2), and are sometimes given direct when the character's choice of words can be made particularly revealing (see p.64, final paragraph).

The incident is a device to demonstrate the decisive qualities Captain Wentworth supposes Anne to be without, and to leave Anne solitary while the rest of her circle seize upon this welcome intrusion by the great world. It also increases the tension of the eventual meeting with the man for whom Anne's 'retentive feelings' unbalance 'all her reasonings'. She cannot help her constancy, she cannot express it, nor would it seem to be desired. To Frederick Wentworth, whose feelings are reported to Mary by the captivated Misses Musgrove, Anne is altered beyond recognition. Characteristically, Anne accepts the severity of this judgement. Frederick Wentworth judges Anne's actions in the past to have been weak and timid. To him she had appeared feeble, and had been a deep disappointment which his attachment had not deserved. At this stage unforgiving, he is simply uninterested in her, and, ironically, intends to marry 'a strong mind with sweetness of manner'.

brother Charles, her brother-in-law.
unsuspicious i.e. Mary is unaware that she is hurting Anne in any particular way by what she reports.
nice Fastidious or particular – the eighteenth century meaning of the word.

Chapter 8

Although Captain Wentworth and Anne Elliot meet frequently they observe the obligatory formalities only. The officer's conversation and stories inspire the interest and affection of the young women. Anne Elliot's role is to play the piano at the gatherings, and she is thankful to be unobserved.

Commentary

The point of view reverts to Anne's, excluded as she is from the 'merry, joyous party'. Captain Wentworth's charm and vitality are strongly felt as, prompted by his sister and the admiral, he talks about his adventures. This sailor is a compelling, fascinating creature to ladies who live close to the 'idle refinement' to which Mrs Croft has refused to be condemned.

the year six 1806.
interest No connections to help his career.
at that time Frederick refers obliquely to the sorrow Anne's decision had caused him.
taking privateers Capturing enemy merchant ships, commissioned and armed in war-time.
French frigate A large vessel to be captured by a sloop.
Sound Plymouth Sound.
Great Nation France; a sardonic reference to the French styling themselves thus.
How fast I made money in her i.e. prize money, by successive captures of enemy vessels.
assizes Mr Musgrove's journeys are to the county town, for the visit of the circuit judge.

Chapter 9

Charles Hayter, the eldest of the Musgroves' cousins returns to Uppercross after a fortnight's absence. Henrietta and Charles have seemed to be attached to one another, but no formal engagement has been proposed. Charles is disquieted to observe that Captain Wentworth may be a potential rival. Mary Musgrove speculates on the likelihood of a match between the Captain and Henrietta. Captain Wentworth calls at Uppercross unexpectedly, finding Anne alone with the invalid Charles; Charles Hayter appears almost immediately and an awkward situation is made worse until Captain Wentworth's instinctive kindness moves him to help Anne with the children.

Commentary

The chapter is a blend of sharply observed attitudes and manners, domestic comedy, and sentiments delicately drawn. Charles Hayter's 'pretensions' are an affront to Mary, who considers herself the 'principal' part of the Musgrove family. Charles Musgrove will be satisfied with an equable and profitable distribution of suitors between his sisters.

Mary Musgrove's assessment of Charles Hayter's suitability as a prospective husband for Henrietta is an interesting example of Elliot thinking. Education and manners must be weighed against the absence of property and connection. Henrietta is about to throw herself away, much as Lady Russell, less frivolously, had thought Anne was doing in the past. Charles Musgrove gives a rational counterpoint of the expectations that make his cousin a respectable suitor for Henrietta. Her parents see Henrietta's feelings as being more important than a 'match' (p.78, paragraph 2), and Anne, appealed to as arbiter in discussions, yet, we presume, playing no part, is possibly not alone in the realistic and unsentimental opinion that happiness is a practical possibility. Thematically the discussion is significant; the basis for an irrevocable personal decision is the subject of debate, notwithstanding its fragmentary form and the petty domesticity of its tone.

The final scene of Wentworth's rescue of Anne emphasizes the silence between them, the tension that still exists, and a depth to Anne's feelings of which she is scarcely aware herself.

all the charms . . . upon credit Frederick has yet to visit his brother, the curate, to be introduced to his wife.

dependencies Their family, particularly the daughters and cousins.

new creation A new baronetcy did not confer the same distinction as an old one.

getting something from the Bishop i.e. obtaining a living, perhaps becoming a vicar.

teaze Play with or disturb.

Chapter 10

Louisa arranges a walk to Winthrop so that Henrietta and Charles Hayter may perhaps be reconciled. Anne inadvertently overhears Captain Hayter complimenting Louisa on her strength of character in persuading her sister to call on the Hayters. Later Anne is grateful for Captain Wentworth's discreet insistence that she should return to Uppercross in the admiral's gig.

Commentary

The 'long' walk is engineered by Louisa so that Henrietta can present herself, silently penetential, to Charles Hayter, who has astutely buried himself in books. Anne perceives that Louisa, not Henrietta, is the favourite, and this is confirmed by events. Captain Wentworth fervently approves of Louisa's firmness – she prefers to be overturned by the man of her choice than driven safely by another, and is promoting her own interest by helping Henrietta. Frederick's wish to approve 'fortitude' and 'strength of mind' is, by implication, as admirable as it is misplaced. We continue to see him through Anne's eyes – hence the necessity for the eavesdropping scene. Frederick's interest in Anne, conscious or not, may be inferred from the intensity of his admiration of Louisa's spirit, from his curiosity to know more of Anne's refusal to marry Charles Musgrove, and from his concern at her fatigue. Anne has been cordially invited, as a guardian and protectress to the Musgrove girls, after Mary has crassly ignored signs that they would prefer privacy. She occupies herself with reflections of seasonal melancholy. She suffers the fate of being a listener most of the day, and with particular anguish when she overhears but cannot answer Louisa's comment that it was Lady Russell who had persuaded Anne not to marry Charles Musgrove.

The substance of the chapter is complex and emotional; the prevailing tone is rational and for the most part playful. The feelings themselves are not exempt from ironic scrutiny; as nothing else can present itself, the 'sweets of poetic despondence' are enjoyed. Less intricately but equally to the point, Mary's rampant snobbery almost foils the Musgroves' best-laid plans, whilst Charles and the admiral succeed in becoming parodies of themselves: the one darting into a hedge to hunt a weasel, the other nearly losing a wheel of his carriage as he enthuses over the indistinguishable Misses Musgrove.

admired i.e. wondered at.
sweets of poetical despondence The solace of a romantic indulgence of sorrow.
hedge-row A small border area of woodland. See J.E. Austen-Leigh's *A Memoir of Jane Austen*, Chapter 20.
sitting down together i.e. as man and wife.
spread a little more canvas Hurry up – the Admiral's nautical metaphor.

Revision questions on Chapters 6–10

1 Describe life at Uppercross.

2 What do we learn of the Hayters?

3 What evidence is there that Captain Wentworth is attracted to Louisa?

4 What do we learn of Captain Wentworth's naval career?

5 Indicate, in some detail, the role or roles played by Anne in these chapters.

Chapter 11

Anticipating her return to Kellynch Lodge with Lady Russell, Anne is unexpectedly taken to Lyme Regis in company with Louisa and Henrietta, Mary and Charles, and Captain Wentworth.

Commentary

The chapter introduces new characters and opens the hitherto closed circle of Kellynch – Uppercross, allowing Anne's virtue to be seen in action. The setting is important in its exciting novelty, especially to Louisa and Henrietta and, in its autumnal atmosphere, to Anne and Captain Benwick. Mourning the loss of his fiancée, the serious-minded Benwick is regarded by Anne as less unfortunate than herself. This is not self-pity: his love is dead, he is free, and a man. Her former love is alive and now before her constantly; she is a woman, confined. Anne expects and encourages Captain Benwick to recover from his misfortune, to read for 'moral and religious' inspiration, and not merely for emotional consolation. Her judgement of his indulgence in the seductions of romantic refinement is stern, but relieved by a hint of ironic self-depreciation in recognizing her own tendency to the same fault.

rooms The public assembly rooms.
Cobb The old stone pier at Lyme.
give-and-take invitations i.e. formal invitations.
Marmion **or** *The Lady of the Lake* Poems by Sir Walter Scott (1771–1832).
Giaour **and** *The Bride of Abydos* Poems by Lord Byron (1788–1824).
our best moralists Dr Johnson, for example.

Chapter 12

Henrietta talks to Anne about her hopes that the curacy at Uppercross might fall vacant. A gentleman, who is later discovered to be Mr William Walter Elliot, notices Anne. Captain Harville thanks Anne for giving her companionship to Captain Benwick. Louisa falls from the Cobb and is assumed to be seriously ill. Arrangements are made for Louisa to remain in Lyme and to be nursed by Mrs Harville. Mary insists on remaining with her, despite the general wish that Anne should do so. Captain Wentworth conducts Henrietta and Anne to Uppercross to break the news to Louisa's parents.

Commentary

To Anne the accident on the Cobb is the result of wilfulness without 'proportions and limits' (see Anne's reflections p.112). Because of her naturally considerate disposition, her resilience and her decisiveness, it is Anne who is ready to give the lead in this crisis. Captain Wentworth's declaration that there is 'no one so proper, so capable as Anne' is thwarted by Mary's insistence on being centre stage.

Even before the incident, Anne is an emergent figure. Henrietta's confiding in her her hopes of Charles Hayter's succeeding Dr Shirley – and therefore the possibility of her marriage to Charles – is consistent with Anne as 'listener'; Captain Harville's expression of his gratitude for Anne's perceptive response to his friend's disquieting state of mind suggests an infinitely less passive role; and the spontaneous admiration of the unknown gentleman (noticed by Captain Wentworth), is an indication of the effect that company and activity have on Anne. She is becoming, once again, a person of interest.

procuring a dispensation i.e. obtaining the Bishop's permission to become an absentee clergyman.

entering into the feelings . . . a young man i.e. Anne sympathizes with Henrietta in her anxiety as she had done with Captain Benwick in his grief.

baronight Unintentionally comic pronunciation.

arms Coat-of arms, indicating Elliot ancestry, which would have been on the side of the coach.

made into Promoted to Captain of.

run up to the yard-arm A punishment at sea.

did think on the question with perfect decision i.e. an ironic understatement. Anne is greatly moved by Captain Harville's account.

dark blue sea A reference to Byron's famous narrative poem 'Childe Harold'.

jump Catch her, or help her jump down.

time required by the Uppercross horses The coach would take longer than a chaise.

sister i.e. by marriage.

Emma . . . Henry In the ballad 'Henry and Emma' by Matthew Prior (1664 – 1721), Emma is prepared to serve the woman she thinks Henry loves.

baited Fed, refreshed.

Chapter 13

Anne stays two days with Mr and Mrs Musgrove. Due to leave for Kellynch with Lady Russell, she encourages Louisa's parents to travel to Lyme themselves. Lady Russell and Anne talk of the events at Lyme, and pay a visit to Kellynch Hall to see Admiral and Mrs Croft.

Commentary

Anne is thankful to be freed from any immediate likelihood of seeing Captain Wentworth at Kellynch, the scene of their first meetings, or in company with Lady Russell. His return to Lyme, and the Crofts' intention to travel north to visit relations, effectively leave her alone with precious recollections of Uppercross and some 'breathings of friendship and reconciliation', which, she supposes, could never be looked for again.

blains Blisters, boils, chilblains.
misty glasses i.e. the windows of Lady Russell's carriage.
cousin Mr Elliot.
by nature Aware that her thoughts are at Lyme, Anne feels that she ought to be thinking of her father and sister.
awkwardness . . . must speak Lady Russell and Anne must at some point speak of Captain Wentworth.
a note Captain Wentworth is keeping her informed (see p.117).
intelligence News.
This was handsome Anne's reported reflection on Captain Wentworth's compliment.

Chapter 14

Charles and Mary return from Lyme, bringing news of Louisa's recovery and an account of Captain Benwick's apparent interest in Anne. Whilst Louisa remains convalescing at Lyme, and Henrietta with her, Mr and Mrs Musgrove celebrate a family Christmas with their own younger children and the Harville children. Anne hears from Elizabeth that Mr Elliot is at Bath, and soon she is taken there herself by Lady Russell.

Commentary

The tone of the narrative is almost seasonal. Mary's visit to Lyme had been successful. Charles's impression is that Captain Benwick is becoming attached to Anne, and this idea is strengthened in the reader's mind by Mary's hostility to it, but it is unconfirmed. Captain Benwick does not appear.

Anne's vitality, the return of her youthful bloom and spirits, is stressed ironically, by Mary's dismissal of any such possibility and, more delicately, by Anne's response to Captain Benwick's attentions, and by her acknowledging to herself that she would rather see Mr Elliot than not.

a struggle on each side . . . hospitable i.e. the Musgroves and the Harvilles were each trying to do the best for one another.
Mary had had her evils i.e. she had found things to complain of.
library The circulating library. Books were borrowed on subscription.
bathed See Ch.11, p.95 bathing machines. Ladies and gentlemen

bathed from a 'machine' or cart, in which they undressed and were towed into the water. This pursuit was thought to be health-giving.

when one drops one's scissors Mary expects a gentleman to be perfectly attentive to a lady.

paid their compliments Called upon the Musgroves.

a fine family-piece Appreciative, yet ironic. The scene is a typical noisy, confused family gathering.

drays Low carts.

pattens Wooden soles on an iron ring, to keep the shoe from the ground in wet weather.

smoking in rain To the country dweller, the large number of coal-fired chimneys would give this unusual effect.

Revision questions on Chapters 11–14

1 Describe the Harvilles and their home.

2 Describe the development of Anne's friendship with Captain Benwick.

3 What are the immediate results of Louisa's accident? What arrangements are subsequently made?

4 Write a character study of Mary as she appears in these chapters.

Chapter 15

Anne joins her father and her sister at Bath, and is introduced to Mr Elliot.

Commentary

Sir Walter and Elizabeth, delighted with Bath and with themselves, are glad to welcome a captive audience. Sir Walter and Elizabeth being what they are, the behaviour of Mr William Walter Elliot and his reconciliation with the family is regarded cautiously by Anne – until she is impressed by his 'sensible discerning mind', gentlemanly bearing and sympathetic interest in the family's affairs. Again the reader is offered the central character's view, necessarily limited, of another character. The chapter begins with promise of 'imprisonment' in 'littleness', attended by the inane excitement of the baronet and his daughter, and ends with pleasurable reflections on the society of Mr Elliot. Bath may not be what it seems.

an advantage i.e. the table was now formally complete.

laying out for compliments i.e. hinting broadly that they wished to be told that they were missed at Kellynch.

cards left In practical terms cards, bearing the visitor's name, were left when a visitor called and found no one at home. Socially, leaving cards came to mean the expression of an interested in beginning or strengthening an acquaintance.

he had passed through Bath in November This is explained later (Ch.21, p.180).

unfeudal i.e. unsympathetic to the traditional role of the aristocracy and gentry.

no dinners in general i.e. they were not in the habit of inviting numbers of guests.

sensible i.e. aware.

under-hung i.e. his chin was prominent.

one person's manners i.e. Captain Wentworth's.

must not be i.e. ought not to be.

'silver sounds' Recalling Pope, *The Rape of the Lock*, Canto I, 'And the press'd watch returned a silver sound.'

watchman Nightwatchmen walked the town at night, calling out the hours. They were the forerunners of the police force.

Chapter 16

Anne fears Sir Walter's attachment to Mrs Clay, and Mr Elliot confides his disapproval of it. Lady Russell comes to admire Mr Elliot, and imagines that his attentions to the family are inspired by an interest in the younger daughter. For her part, Anne is altogether more cautious. The Dowager Viscountess Dalrymple and her daughter, distant relatives of the Elliots, arrive in Bath, and Sir Walter and Elizabeth are eager to arrange an intro-duction.

Commentary

'Family connexions' and attitudes to them are the themes of the chapter. Anne fears that Sir Walter may marry Mrs Clay. This would make the lady mistress of Kellynch; an heir would make things worse, particularly for the myopic Elizabeth. Lady Russell abhors the association with Mrs Clay, not only because it is 'out of place', but she also feels deeply the slights to Anne that are unceasingly given by the Elliots' conduct. Lady Russell's judge-ment of Mr Elliot as a suitable connection is questioned by implication; Anne has known the judgement of her 'excellent friend' to be faulty. One or other of them has misjudged, and possibly in more than one way. Anne takes marriage to Elizabeth to be Mr Elliot's concern. She admits that his respect for rank and social niceties would always direct his intentions, formally at least, first to Elizabeth, and therefore they might, in practice, disguise the truth. Anne suspends judgement; Lady Russell is already persuaded. With regard to Mr Elliot personally, the narrative is tantalizingly vague. He is described as he is seen, by Lady Russell largely, with Anne's discreet suspicions as an intriguing question mark. Even Anne respects him sufficiently to speak openly to him, to argue with him over the definition of 'place', a matter which emphasizes their differences significantly.

On the subject of good company, intelligence and cultivation are proposed by Anne, and tentatively admitted by Mr Elliot as not being quite a disadvantage, being less important to him than family connection and an appropriate manner, This, to Anne, is taking the shadow for the substance, appearance for reality. The discussion is light-hearted in tone and treatment, and occasioned by the appearance of the Dalrymples, and the Elliots' fawning pursuit of three lines of scrawl. It is a discussion that divides the family, as do intelligence and temperament. Anne differs from everyone else, in greater or lesser degree, in that she is content to be 'nobody', if she can have what she values. The pride of Sir Walter and Elizabeth is demonstrably vanity, Anne's is self-respect. Anne is ashamed of her father's veneration for society. Strength of character and sureness of judgement are attractive in themselves, and Mr Elliot, as Lady Russell evidently believes, may well be captivated by the very indignation that he has inspired. Even Sir Walter notices Anne's improved looks, enhanced as they must be by her ease and growing confidence.

Gowland A skin lotion of the day.
freckles Sir Walter appears to be convincing himself that Mrs Clay's blemishes (see Ch.5, p.47) have disappared.
evil of the marriage . . . marry i.e. at least Elizabeth would then in her own right be mistress of a household.
drinks the water The waters were supposed to have invigorating properties.
the others Elizabeth and Sir Walter.
the future i.e. Lady Russell is hinting at the possibility that Mr Elliot may wish to court Anne.
crape i.e. a black band, indicating that the wearer is in mourning.

dissolved i.e. ended, by his wife's death.
another person's look i.e. Captain Wentworth's.
letters of ceremony Formal communications, for example
  acknowledgement of births, deaths, and marriages.
compromise of propriety Any demeaning attentions.
a little learning A reference to Pope's *An Essay on Criticism*.
place Social position.
great acquaintance Becoming acquainted with persons of high rank.
her Mrs Clay.

Chapter 17

Anne calls on Mrs Smith, a former school friend, now a widow, in poor health and straitened circumstances. Lady Russell is by now convinced that Anne ought to accept Mr Elliot, should he eventually propose marriage.

Commentary

Mrs Smith adds no obvious complication to the plot at this point, but what she has to say about human nature in adversity is thematically relevant. Mrs Smith, friendless, virtually crippled and barely able to earn a living, has the 'good sense and agreeable manners' which Anne might well have remembered. More than this, in a profoundly depressing situation, Mrs Smith is resilient rather than resigned. It is her 'power' of finding or creating 'good' where everything is against it and there is no certainty of any reward for self-sacrifice and effort that astonishes Anne and excites her admiration.

By choosing this connection, Anne does no more than one expects. Sir Walter and Elizabeth deceive themselves in considering that Mrs Clay's social position is different from that of Mrs Smith, and that her friendship is disinterested. Mrs Smith's experience that 'real' friendship is rare, and that judgements are often irrevocable, their consequences irreversible, is an understanding from which Sir Walter's and Elizabeth's philosophy excludes them. It has a direct bearing on Anne's position when she hears the siren voice of Lady Russell's bewitching persuasion. Mr Elliot's imperfections are invisible to Lady Russell, and she urges Anne to consider assuming her mother's place as the mistress of Kellynch Hall. The emotional power of the suggestion and all that it evokes, together with the wish to delight her closest friend, momentarily beguile her. But Mr Elliot's guarded performance, attractive though it is, is suspect, and his worth unproven. The past, and what is not known about it, is enough to counsel prudence.

pushing . . . Laura-place i.e. busy associating themselves with the Dalrymples.
governess See Ch.2, p.32.
as Anne chose i.e. as Anne would permit. (See p.142) She does not wish to advertise herself by arriving in a grand carriage.
almost ventured to depend upon Which she had expected to find.
dissipations A reference to the life Mrs Smith had led with her husband. (See Ch.21, p.176).
disinterested i.e. selfless; not seeking any personal advantage.
au fait Up-to-date.
Miss Anne Elliot Sir Walter speaks of her in the third person to emphasize her standing as his daughter.
no honours No addition to the coat-of-arms as a mark of special distinction.
theirs Their friend, Mrs Clay.
desirableness In social and material terms it would be an ideal match for Anne.
with propriety i.e. he is still in mourning for his wife.
Sunday-travelling Implying a casual observance of religious duty.

Chapter 18

The Crofts arrive in Bath, bringing a letter from Mary, which informs Anne that Captain Benwick and Louisa Musgrove are to be married. Meeting the admiral by chance, Anne tries to discover what might be Captain Wentworth's feeling about his friend's courtship of Louisa.

Commentary

The letter tells the reader a great deal about Mary. Offering an erratic evaluation of what it conveys, it introduces important developments that have occurred earlier and elsewhere, leaving us to imagine the recipient's reaction. The comedy of Mary, self-pitying and wildly inconsistent, precedes Anne's consideration of the news. The affectionate officer had had to find someone to love, and the presence of Louisa Musgrove's youthful charm and vivacity coincided with his mood of romantic tenderness. Confused by her delight at the prospect of Captain

Wentworth not marrying Louisa Musgrove, Anne nevertheless does her best to prise from Admiral Croft any information he may have about Frederick. Quite unconscious of Anne's anxiety, the admiral tells her that Frederick's letter to his sister breathed not a word of reproach for the man who was to carry off 'Miss (what's her name?)'. Anne does not know what to think.

convenient passports Sir Walter imagines that the Crofts are carrying the letters so that they may introduce themselves to the Elliots at Bath.

consequence Significance; because the rain makes the lanes muddy, travel difficult, and is restricting of society.

to offer to take anything i.e. letters, for example.

as long as I like Weight does not matter, since no postage will be due.

agreeable Mary thinks that Captain Benwick will be less interested now in books and churches.

an interesting state A romantic figure, recovering as she was from a serious accident.

sensible If it were possible for Louisa to love another, having once admired Captain Wentworth, then in itself the engagement to Captain Benwick is nothing remarkable.

printshop Selling drawings.

cockleshell Small, makeshift boat.

Shabby fellows i.e. in behaviour; see several lines later.

younker Young man. The peace had come too soon for Sir Drew's grandson as it takes away the opportunity of making his career and fortune.

Sophys A simple old-fashioned name, like his wife's.

Edward Frederick's brother Edward, Mr Wentworth the curate.

bears i.e. has.

soft Quiet, unassuming. (piano).

augur want of spirit Infer a lack of spirit.

did not receive the perfect conviction Remained unconvinced.

Revision questions on Chapters 15–18

1 What do we learn of the house in Camden-place, and the life led there by Sir Walter and Elizabeth?

2 How is Mr Elliot made to seem attractive to Anne? What are her reservations about him?

3 Describe the circumstances in which Mrs Smith finds herself.

4 Note the reactions of the Elliots to the arrival in Bath of the Dalrymples.

5 Write a detailed commentary on Mary's letter. What effect(s) does it have on Anne?

Chapter 19

Anne meets Captain Wentworth, who appears embarrassed at seeing her and uneasy talking to her. Mr Elliot, whom Captain Wentworth recognizes, is escorting Anne. Anxious to speak further with Frederick and to know his feelings about Louisa's forthcoming marriage to Captain Benwick, Anne looks forward to a concert to which the Elliots are invited, and which he may attend.

Commentary

The wrangle over who should ride in the Dalrymples' carriage is more than it seems. Mr Elliot wishes to be left to escort Anne, and Mrs Clay wishes to be left to be escorted by Mr Elliot.

The first meeting, since Lyme, of Anne and Captain Wentworth is awkward, with the unease on this occasion being mainly Frederick's: 'Time had changed him, or Louisa had changed him', and this is all that Anne can imagine. Mr Elliot's familiar manner and his attentiveness to Anne make public what the chorus of ladies divines, and Anne's 'gentle and embarrassed glance' is, ironically, inadvertent confirmation. Mrs Smith's enigmatic comment at the end of the chapter completes the puzzle. Anne and Captain Wentworth cannot meet privately; the street or the 'elegant stupidity' of social gatherings are the only opportunities for escaping the 'stagnation'. Frederick is now trapped in the convention that has almost suffocated Anne. Desperately seeking some means of communicating with him, Anne can only do so indirectly, and circumstances convey the contrary of what she intends. In a world of public intercourse, behaviour must be interpreted imperfectly.

Molland's A shop.
barouche Fashionable four-wheeled carriage, with a canopy.
betraying the least sensibility i.e. Anne felt that she was more in command of herself than he was.
arch significance i.e. special meaning, possibly wry amusement.
chair Sedan chair.
party Company; we do not know whom. They serve as a chorus.

drew back her head i.e. they appear to be in Lady Russell's carriage.
answer Prove a success.

Chapter 20

At the concert Captain Wentworth tells Anne of his surprise at Captain Benwick's marrying Louisa. Anne realizes that his feelings towards her may have changed. Mr Elliot's purposeful attentiveness thwarts Anne's intention to speak further, and Captain Wentworth leaves, apparently jealous.

Commentary

The almost too interesting conversation makes plain that Captain Wentworth is in love with Anne. In praising the Musgroves, he unintentionally refers to the past and reveals the strength of his feelings about Sir Walter's inadequacy as a parent, and what he sees as the misguided interference of Lady Russell; and in his comments on Captain Benwick's love for Fanny Harville he implies respect for constancy, indeed a belief in it. If Captain Benwick ought not to recover from such devotion, then neither can Captain Wentworth. Frederick's open nature makes the conversation one of hesitant self-declaration, the more moving for being without art or premeditation. Anne's replies are as indirect as Frederick's statements. Referring obliquely to the past, she declares that the pain of loss cannot be regretted unless the happiness is also to be denied. The precarious intimacy of these exchanges is already threatened by the intrusive setting and the 'ceaseless' harassment of social obligation when Mr Elliot intervenes with what to Anne is incalculably ill-effect. Seeming to confirm an attachment hinted at by earlier circumstances, the unwelcome enthusiasm of Mr Elliot for her Italian is enough to provoke Captain Wentworth's abrupt departure. Anne is left to ponder what has been left unsaid by Captain Wentworth, and what has been said by Mr Elliot – that he wishes her name may never change, and his inference that he has known of her for longer than she can imagine. With flattery and mystery on one side, and the masking of truth on the other, the drama is in the urge to speak and the impossibility of doing so. The public assembly rooms are the noisy, pretentious background for tentative revelation. Confusion and misinterpretation separate those whom the past has already divided.

perhaps Captain Wentworth's comments on the Musgroves are
  retrospectively criticism of Anne's family. She realizes this, and he
  breaks off as he also becomes aware of the comparison.
nothing of the matter i.e. Mr Elliot uses heavy irony in flattering.
might never change If Anne were to marry him, she would remain an
  Elliot.
the gapes Yawning, boredom.
Miss Larolles A self-assertive character in the novel *Cecilia* by Fanny
  Burney.

Chapter 21

Having discovered that she is mistaken in thinking that Anne
intends to marry Mr Elliot, Mrs Smith tells her all she knows of
him. A friend of her husband, he encouraged the latter's finan-
cial excesses, and was indifferent to his ruin and later to the
plight of his widow. Mrs Smith also tells Anne what she has
heard from Nurse Rooke, which is that Mr Elliot's view of a
baronetcy has altered, and he now covets the title. Accordingly,
he is in Bath to observe, and if possible to thwart, any plans Mrs
Clay may have to marry Sir Walter. His interest in Anne is
genuine, however.

Commentary

A chapter of revelation is sustained by the contrivances of Mrs
Smith's history and Nurse Rooke's discoveries. Unconvincing
though the structure of this narrative may seem to be, as a series
of coincidences, externally imposed, and an insertion rather
than an episode in the continuous development of the story, the
effect is still dramatic. Even allowing for the 'unqualified bitter-
ness' of Mrs Smith, her evidence is ample proof that Mr Elliot is
demonstrably 'deficient both in justice and compassion'. His
guiding principle is selfishness, and his iniquitous conduct in the
past explains what Anne found unconvincing about his recent
behaviour, and shows her what she might have allied herself
with, had she yielded to Lady Russell's persuasion. The revela-
tions dramatize the validity of Anne's loyalty to an ideal.

much to regret i.e. Mr Elliot's presence and manner had led Captain
  Wentworth to conclude that Anne was about to become engaged to
  him.
the mistake Mrs Smith supposed 'the person who interests you' to be

Mr Elliot; Anne had thought she meant Captain Wentworth.

worn out The friendship has ceased.

premature In anticipating the marriage between Mr Elliot and Anne, before it has been formally announced.

Temple One of the four Inns of Court. He was probably training for the bar.

very different creature from . . . Mrs Smith was going to say 'Elizabeth'.

pretend to Make an attempt to.

to the hammer To auction.

reversion i.e. inheritance. (The estate reverting to the next male in line in the family).

artificial Artful, cunning.

embarrassments enough . . . their friends i.e. they had been obliged to borrow money.

sequestration i.e. the estate was held in lieu of payment of certain debts or taxes. When these were paid, the estate would be freed and therefore could be sold.

Chapter 22

Mr Elliot's presence is now offensive to Anne, and she is pleased to hear that he is leaving Bath temporarily. Charles and Mary arrive in Camden place. They are staying at the White Hart with Mrs Musgrove and Henrietta. Captain Harville has travelled with them. When Anne calls at the White Hart to see her friends, Captain Wentworth enters with Captain Harville. Mary draws the attention of the company to Mr Elliot, who is in conversation with Mrs Clay. Anne is embarrassed by this, and is glad to speak briefly but privately with Captain Wentworth. They are interrupted by the arrival of Sir Walter and Elizabeth. Anne's innate distrust of Mr Elliot is now compounded by legitimate abhorrence of his conduct to Mrs Smith. The immediate problem is the continuing deception of Lady Russell, Sir Walter and Elizabeth. The selflessness of Anne's nature is also seen in her approval of the Musgroves' sincerity and parental concern for their children's welfare, and her happiness for Henrietta in her good fortune.

Commentary

This is a time of acute suspense for Anne. Mr Elliot's pursuit, hopeless as it is, may nevertheless alienate Captain Wentworth.

Naturally unassuming, living in and accepting rigidly defined conventions, she cannot assert herself in her own interest without demeaning the fineness of sensibility that gives her 'elegance of mind'. She is no more able to speak of personal constancy to Captain Wentworth than she feels free to warn her family of their involvement with a man of whom she disapproves. She depends entirely on opportunity; it is Mrs Musgrove's insistent and considerate respect that offers Anne the chance to declare herself before Captain Wentworth. The squabble over a choice of entertainment gives Anne a chance to express her opinion, and she can then indirectly declare her disinterest in the gathering to which Mr Elliot is invited. The conversation between Anne and Captain Wentworth which follows, on time and constancy, is as private as mirrors, china and cards allow, and its life is too easily extinguished by 'cold composure, determined silence or insipid talk'.

spell Hint.
to hold a living . . . under many years i.e. Charles Hayter has been offered the position and income of rector of a parish, which he will hold temporarily until the young man for whom it is intended is ordained.
the best preserves in the kingdom i.e. ideal country for the sportsman.
coming down with money . . . it streightens him i.e. Mr Musgrove has the expense of marrying off two daughters at the same time.
Usefulness At Lyme.
wonted Usual.
Anne talked of being perfectly ready . . . pity her i.e. had Henrietta known of Anne's reluctance to leave, she would have understood and sympathized.
her jealous eyes i.e. her close observation.

Chapter 23

The next morning at the Musgroves' rooms, Captain Wentworth is present when Anne arrives. Captain Harville and Anne discuss the relative constancy of men and women. Realizing belatedly that Captain Wentworth may be listening to the conversation, Anne is drawn to make an indirect but unmistakable statement of her feelings. Captain Wentworth, supposedly writing a letter to Captain Benwick on Captain Harville's behalf, surreptitiously hands Anne the letter he has in fact been composing, which declares the strength of his own affections, and asks for some confirmation of Anne's. Captain Wentworth having left the room already, Anne must follow him. Charles Musgrove insists on accompanying her, but on their meeting Captain Wentworth, he leaves. Free to speak, Anne and Captain Wentworth resolve misunderstandings, and he gives a history of his mistakes and his consequent suffering.

Commentary

At the White Hart Anne's happiness at being in the presence of Captain Wentworth is qualified, in a statement of ironic antithesis, by the misery of knowing nothing for certain. The conversation between Mrs Croft and Mrs Musgrove turns to engagements, and Mrs Croft's definition of prudence in this context is one that applies retrospectively and affirmatively to Anne's breaking off her engagement to Captain Wentworth. Anne and Frederick are aware of the discussion. An unspoken dialogue begins. To what extent it continues during Anne's conversation with Captain Harville is initially left vague. Captain Wentworth is 'not very near' as Anne describes the emotionally vulnerable predicament of women living 'at home, quiet, confined'. Recognizing the demands of a sailor's life specifically, with 'neither time, nor health, nor life' he can call his own, she adds, faltering with depth of emotion, that even finer sensibilities would be unendurable. As she becomes more aware of her audience, still speaking passionately and sincerely in answer to Captain Harville's equally deeply felt argument, she is able, while generalizing to Captain Harville, to speak before Captain Wentworth the truth of her continuing to love, even when hope is gone.

A discreetly proffered letter of reciprocation is all that public gaze permits. The suspense is increased by the urgency of the obligation to reply clearly to the letter's request for a sign that Captain Wentworth has not again misunderstood. The emotional qualities of the scene are modified ironically as Anne's reaction is variously interpreted as some disabling complaint, and by her propulsion home in the company of Charles, earnestly and, fortunately temporarily, sacrificing his sporting interests in order to escort her. This prepares the reader for the emotionally restrained report of the reconciliation, where a more immediate relation of events would have been intrusive and possibly cloying in its inevitable sentimentality (see cancelled chapter), and is a finely balanced epilogue to the drama of blind utterance via an intermediary quite unaware of the significance of his role.

Retrospection follows and the story is retold as Captain Wentworth has known it. Apart from the reference to 'over-persuasion' (Chapter 7, p.68) and the statement there that 'Her power with him was gone for ever', the reader's perception of events has been Anne's. That earlier statement of Captain Wentworth's feelings is now revealed to have been unreliable, true only to his incomplete understanding of himself. Having 'learnt to distinguish between the steadiness of principle and the obstinacy of self-will', Captain Wentworth's judgement is gradually aligned with Anne's, the author's and therefore by implication the reader's. Frederick's narrative of his 'penance' and their discussion of persuasion is continued in part in direct speech. The subject matter is crucial, the characters' attitudes central; because all is known, and emotions are relatively stable, thought and judgement resume their pre-eminence. In the greenhouse atmosphere of a gathering of 'those who had never met before, and those who had met too often' there is vitality in the snatched exchanges. Frederick's ironic self-depreciating admissions relieve Anne and even Lady Russell of the final responsibility for the 'division and estrangement', and Anne's calm assertions of principle imply that she is more exquisitely happy precisely because of her refusal to blur the distinction between what she wanted to do and what she felt she ought to do.

one quarter i.e. its effects on Captain Wentworth.
an alloy i.e. Anne's exultation is so heady that she is glad to reassure
  herself of its reality by 'momentary apprehensions' and thus
  strengthen her happiness.

Chapter 24

The chapter summarizes the characters' differing reactions to the marriage of Anne Elliot and Captain Wentworth.

Commentary

The conclusion is that perseverance is its own persuasion, 'bad morality but . . . the truth' as the pronominal narrator believes. The lovers have every advantage now: 'maturity of mind, consciousness of right, and one independent fortune' are more than sufficient to withstand what is largely the unconcern of the family, graceless as it nonetheless is for that. The purity of Elliot folly is sardonically illustrated here as a compound of personal vanity, self-absorption and pettiness. Anne's only sense of inferiority with regard to her husband is keenly felt: 'the consciousness of having no relations to bestow on him which a man of sense could value'.

Like Captain Wentworth, Lady Russell can learn to accept her errors; she had taken Frederick as being unreliable and impetuous, and Mr Elliot for complete propriety. Her principal virtue is her maternal love for Anne, and this enables her to recover from the tendency to prejudice. The capacity to 'learn' is the element that guarantees her moral survival. Anne is described as being gifted with 'quickness of perception, a nicety of discernment of character, a natural penetration'. This is the writer's view of character: an innate inheritance which may be advanced or abused by adherence to, or neglect of, principle.

Lightness of tone in the references to Sir Walter and Lady Russell give way to the autumnal composure of the later perception of Lady Russell, and of Anne's grief at the manifest spiritual poverty of her closest relations. Mr Elliot and Mrs Clay are to be rewarded perhaps with each other, and by contrast, Mrs Smith is rewarded with friendship, health, and the recovery of her property. Finally, 'felicity' is defined as tenderness, and a security threatened only by unavoidable exigencies of fate.

personal claims i.e. his appearance.
the volume of honour Debrett's *Peerage*.
the nights of seniority i.e. Mary had taken precedence over Anne, her elder sister, while the latter was unmarried.
landaulette A small landau; a four-wheeled carriage, seating four people, with an adjustable canopy.
under his protection i.e. as his mistress.

Revision questions on Chapters 19–24

1 Summarize Mrs Smith's story. What part does it play in the plot of the novel?

2 What arguments are put forward by Captain Harville and Anne during their discussion at the White Hart?

3 Summarize the account Captain Wentworth finally gives of all that has happened to him.

Jane Austen's art in *Persuasion*
The characters

Anne Elliot

'elegance of mind and sweetness of character'

Persuasion is a novel of character, its subject being the nature of an individual who must choose and therefore judge. Anne Elliot is the central character, whose sensibilities deepen, whose understanding of reality is necessarily limited by circumstances, but whose judgement does not falter. Other characters may perceive incorrectly, and their judgement, in so far as they are capable of it, is educated. Anne endures, having to find her inner strength in a world that initially denies her fulfilment.

The central character with whose perception the reader is aligned is the focal point from which other characters are observed. The narrative is an implicit commentary made to a reader who, it may be deduced, receives or shares the ideas that are either Anne's views, or judgements of character with which she would agree. The intensity of the presentation of Anne's character derives from her aloneness. 'Only' Anne, she is not thought of by her immediate family as worth considering or consulting. A silent autumnal figure, she is disregarded by her father, for whom her features can do little to 'excite . . . esteem', and is unwanted by Elizabeth, who thinks Anne's advice as unnecessary as her presence. On the matter of retrenchment she is on 'the side of honesty against importance', and is indifferent to superficial material display. Composing herself, as she must, for an infinity of elegant stupidity, the resurrection of the emotions of the past, intensified by present partiality of vision, is the sweet sorrow of continuous parting. Anne's humanity and humour save her from the fate of a heroine 'almost too good' (from a letter to Fanny Knight, a favourite niece) for her creator. Isolated emotionally and morally, Anne, socially and financially dependent within the cultural and conventional assumptions of the time, is hamstrung, too, by the natural refinement that distinguishes her, from self-assertion that would be a negation of 'elegance of mind and sweetness of character'. She is trapped; but it is her love in action, passionate and idealistic, and not in the preserving fluid of romantic self-absorption, that makes her a reference point for all the other characters who are capable of thought. Her concern for such abstractions as justice and equity stress the importance to her of the necessity for modifying rights by obligations, and the will by duty. Sir Walter and Elizabeth, satirically conceived, do not even possess the sensitivity to be uneasy on such grounds.

Anne talks to her family indirectly, through Lady Russell. In the early chapters most of her words are reported. When she does speak, she is ignored or overruled. She cannot speak to Captain Wentworth. Recollections are perpetually forced on them both, she knows, but nothing is said except in common civility. Her role as more than an unheeded listener does not begin to establish itself until after her release from the confinement of Kellynch. The structure of the novel gradually reverses her position; Lady Russell, Louisa and Henrietta, Charles and Mary, Captain Benwick and Captain Harville, and finally Frederick Wentworth listen to her.

Until the dénouement, her feelings are known only to herself. The full history of her love for Captain Wentworth and his importance in her life are matters jealously guarded. Her private world partially depends for its integrity upon its separation from the formality and compromise of society. The presentation of Anne as always living within herself gives her character a peculiar intuitive accuracy: she senses the form of Mrs Clay's self-advancement, just as she understands its implications; her response to Mary's facile evasion of the tiresome maternal burden of a sick child is tactful and practical; she longs for the power of representing to Captain Wentworth, Henrietta and Louisa what they are allowing themselves to do; her company is sought by Captain Benwick; hardly allowing herself to admit the idea, she knows that there is more to Captain Wentworth's conduct than can be accounted for.

The reference to an early loss of bloom and spirits heighten the sense of the privacy of Anne's experience. She regrets having 'to forego all the influence so sweet and so sad of the autumnal months in the country'. She suffers the departure from Kellynch and the breaking up of the family with 'desolate tranquillity'. On the Winthrop walk Anne manufactures what pleasure she can from 'musings and quotations' on the 'thousand poetical descriptions extant of autumn'. This element of romantic self-indulgence is acknowledged by Anne, and sometimes by the narration. She is amused at finding herself preaching patience to Captain Benwick, ruefully aware that her conduct does not justify her eloquence. She, too, knows the 'happiness of such misery or the misery of such happiness'. Anne is aware of the absurdity of her agitation in the presence of Captain Wentworth; she can laugh at herself at the concert for changing her position on a bench to be within reach of a certain passer-by; capable of pretty 'musings of high-wrought love and eternal constancy', she can smile at Frederick's compliment: 'to my eye you could never alter'. Candour is part of her charm.

Anne's usefulness to others, and how they value it, is a positive measure of their characters. Mary's claims are habitual, and Anne accepts them thankfully for being better than rejection. Mrs Musgrove appeals to her over Mary's spoiling of the children, Louisa and Henrietta over Mary's tenacity in the matter of 'place'; little Charles's accident gives Anne 'everything to do at once – the apothecary to send for – the father to have pursued and informed – the mother to support and keep from hysterics – the servants to control – the youngest child to banish, and the poor suffering one to attend and soothe; – besides sending, as soon as she recollected it, proper notice to the other house, which brought her an accession rather of frightened, enquiring companions, than of very useful assistants'. At Lyme it is 'a very good impulse of her nature' that makes her begin an acquaintance with Captain Benwick when his spirits seem oppressed by the appearance of the party from Uppercross, and it is to Anne that Charles and Captain Wentworth look for direction when they fear that Louisa may be dead.

Anne's reliability in domestic emergencies is an indication of a strength of character that Frederick Wentworth's more extrovert, active idealism does not immediately recognize. Unforgiving, he mistakenly reads weakness and timidity in her character because in his confidence and energy he insists that Anne should judge as he does. He is blind to the truth: 'it was not merely a selfish caution under which she acted . . . Had she not imagined herself consulting his good, even more than her own, she could hardly have given him up.' Anne's rectitude is not an insipid, autumnal morality. The desiccation of Kellynch required 'fortitude' and 'resignation', words Anne uses when thinking of Mrs Smith; but she also values something more: 'that power of turning readily from evil to good, of finding employment which carried her out of herself'.

Her passionate attachment to Captain Wentworth, against her own reasoning, is denied expression; and this suppression of feeling gives emotional concentration to the narrative. Captain Wentworth is introduced by the effect he produces, and the word 'agitation' then appears repeatedly: Anne is anxious that the general ignorance of the past be maintained. She has to steel herself to withstand the Musgrove's gossiping. She is relieved to stay with the injured child, but there is a note of self-pity: 'what was it to her, if Frederick Wentworth were only half a mile distant, making himself agreeable to others!' At one point they are 'actually on the same sofa, divided only by Mrs Musgrove'. The awkwardness of their first meeting alone is further complicated by the arrival of Charles Hayter, and Captain Wentworth's intervening to protect her from her nephew Walter's harassment produces 'most disordered feelings' (Ch.9, p.83). In her apparent invisibility Anne suffers 'extreme agitation' when she overhears Captain Wentworth speaking to Louisa of indecision and idle interference, and listening to what might be his curiosity as to why she refused Charles Musgrove. Without speaking to Anne, Captain Wentworth arranges for her to ride in Admiral Croft's carriage: 'Yes, – he had done it'. Until chance gives her the opportunity to speak, she is almost ridiculously dependent on the interpretation of trifles. When there is something for her to do, the emotion is still strong but the narrative irony is less ambiguous. When she is being driven back to Uppercross from Lyme, Anne is pleased by Captain Wentworth's appeal for her opinion, his deference to her judgement. Calmer, she nevertheless has to compose herself to speak of him to Lady Russell. The news of the engagement of Captain Benwick and Louisa Musgrove is 'almost too wonderful for belief', and when Captain Wentworth tells her of his surprise at it, she has difficulty attending to the concert because of the import of his half-finished sentences. At the White Hart she agonizes over the misconstructions that can be founded on allusions to Mr Elliot, and seizes upon the opening, given by Mrs Musgrove, to distance herself from her cousin. Just after this movement towards Captain Wentworth, the dance of indirect communication is halted by the intrusion of her father and sister, pointedly issuing cards. In each of these instances the effect is comic but at the same time the tension is real, diffused only after the climactic, idealistic 'quarrelling' with Captain Harville, during which Anne claims for her sex the privilege and burden 'of loving longest, when existence or when hope is gone'.

Mr William Walter Elliot is never any threat to this constancy. Anne is natural enough to be flattered by his glance, and 'she felt that she would rather see Mr Elliot again than not', but when she is unable to explain his apparent change of heart, she believes she ought not to trust appearances. Finding him agreeable, and in many respects thinking highly of him (before Mrs Smith's story), she is not convinced that the image is the man: 'And it was not only that her feelings were still adverse to any man save one; her judgement . . . was against Mr Elliot'. Lady Russell's mirage, the idea of Lady Elliot, did affect her imagination and her heart. Reason, and constancy to values, prevailed.

Anne's friendships are permanent and deep, not convenient fabrications like Mr Elliot's, and her respect for 'place' is also strikingly different. She values the individual above the social. She accepts and is grateful for Lady Russell's love, and does not blame her interference. Anne's first concern on learning what Mrs Smith knows of Mr Elliot is to protect her friend from embarrassment. Anne's respect and affection for 'Mrs Smith, such a name!' are incomprehensible to Sir Walter. The Elliots, into whose claustrophobic idiocies Mr Elliot would irrevocably entice Anne, have less pride than she would wish. She tolerates house and dress and furniture, precedence and family connexions, and she sighs to hear Mr Elliot's definition of good company. Far from certain of a future with the man she loves, and quite certain of the dismal prospect of life with Sir Walter and Elizabeth, Anne refuses to consider an alliance without affection, a marriage of convenience. The Elliot pride is self-importance, reflected in what they take for the eyes of the world; Anne's is a self-respecting independence of thought and action.

Anne's sense of duty is sometimes shown in relatively minor ways, and it should not be mistaken for submissiveness. She tries to enlighten Elizabeth, but not because she wishes to or has any hope of success. Her cheerfulness almost cures Mary's hypochondriac boredom. Henrietta confides to Anne her views on the advisability of Dr Shirley's retirement, Anne says 'all that was reasonable and proper' and Henrietta is very well pleased with her companion. When Mary claims her right, as sister-in-law to

Louisa, to stay at Lyme in place of Anne, Anne's submission is reluctant but inevitable. Arriving in Bath, Anne makes herself 'pretend what was proper' to her father and sister, without going so far as to invent compliments about their being regretted at Kellynch. Having heard of Mrs Smith's presence in the town, visiting her is something Anne wants to do because she feels she ought to. She feels 'gratitude and regard, perhaps compassion' for Mr Elliot, after his attentions have caused the incalculable evil of Captain Wentworth's peremptory departure. At the White Hart Charles's declaration that he had smirked and bowed but had not committed himself to meeting Mr Elliot is 'life' to her, but she feels the obligation not to slight her family. She finds Charles's good-natured insistence on taking her home almost cruel, when all she wants to do is find Captain Wentworth, but she will not allow herself to show any feeling but gratitude. These illustrations are comic and ironic in their juxtaposition of Anne's meticulous sense of what is required with the other characters' unawareness of what she is doing. They have a cumulative importance in creating an idealistic, selfless character who manages to avoid seeming pompous or priggish.

Intelligent, honest and kind, Anne is fortunate enough to see more than others do. She suffers for this, but her rewards are greater. She can deny herself happiness because of conscience. The advice of Lady Russell was wrong, as it happened, and because it was founded on uncertainty and distrust it was unwise; the submission to the persuasion, in good faith, was right. Her eventual happiness depended on her willingness to put something else before it.

Captain Wentworth

'a remarkably fine young man, with a great deal of intelligence, spirit and brilliancy'

The reader sees Captain Wentworth entirely through Anne's eyes, and his feelings and intentions are the element of surprise in the love story. These are not wholly known until after the reconciliation with Anne when, in telling his own story, he re-tells the story that has principally been Anne's.

Frederick's continued importance in Anne's life ('a few months more, and *he*, perhaps, may be walking here') is barely understood by Anne and not even suspected by him. He is initially presented in retrospect, as he was when Anne first knew him, his confidence and vitality captivating in its seeming to defy fortune and so control it. Anyone less suited to the enclosure of Kellynch it would be difficult to conceive of. The denial of the freedom and fulfilment which his love had offered Anne produced the 'early loss of bloom and spirits'. The failure of their engagement was, in his judgement, the result of Anne's weakness. When, uniquely, the narrative insight is particularly Frederick's (and from which Anne is excluded), we are told what he thinks, and Anne supposes, and the reader is to be somewhat misled by: 'Her power with him was gone for ever'. His resentment is real enough, and his disposition to fall in love with anyone having exactly Anne's characteristics – 'a strong mind, with sweetness of manner' – is an ironic paradox. The culpability of his folly in encouraging Louisa and Henrietta simultaneously is indefensible, and he almost commits himself to a girl he must have known at the outset is not the 'very superior creature' he can recognize, for example, in Fanny Harville. This is the consequence of his pride and resentment, and his not understanding himself, as he later admits. The positive qualities of honesty, intelligence, sensitivity, sympathy and decisiveness are amply demonstrated by his manner and speech, which are engagingly independent of any intention to move or impress. He is what he seems; he deceives only himself. The evidence is not hard to find. Some of what he does prior to Lyme can be read in two ways: consider the 'studied politeness' before Anne, his silence, his interest in her having refused Charles Musgrove; consider gestures like the removal of Walter, or the arrangement of a seat in a carriage. Later instances are less equivocal: the oddly timed, carefully explained visit to his brother, the glance at a girl who has attracted the glance of a stranger, the insistence, at Lyme, that she is the only fully capable person, the mysterious note or two which finds its way to her.

When the illusion of attachment between Louisa Musgrove and Captain Wentworth is seen for what it has been, Captain Wentworth's comments preface the final section of the book, at Bath, in which he is moving uncertainly towards Anne: 'A man does not recover from such a devotion of the heart to such a woman.' He now knows his real feelings, although neither Anne nor the reader can yet be quite sure of them. 'Anger, resentment, avoidance' have been replaced by the 'friendship . . . regard

... tenderness' of the past. Apparent jealousy of Mr Elliot's familiarity confirms this. The details of Frederick's dual penance are withheld until all uncertainty is resolved, and until after he has written the letter admitting weakness and resentment, and denying inconstancy. His learning to 'distinguish between the steadiness of principle and the obstinacy of self-will' is a balancing of romantic impulse by prudence, a natural conservatism that is not corrupted by personal vanity or social affectation. Understanding precedes suffering: the almost tragic experience of believing that, in his fury, he had probably thrown away what he was searching for is refined by the unavoidable implications of his unguarded friendship with Louisa, and, apparently, the success of a suitor (Mr Elliot) endorsed by influence (Lady Russell). He is honest enough to be amused at the idea of finding himself luckier than he deserves.

Lady Russell

'of sound rather than quick abilities'

Lady Russell is a parent to Anne, and her steadiness of age and character give a conventionality and stability to the life of a 'most dear and highly valued god-daughter, favourite and friend'. The orthodoxy of Lady Russell is not the sham 'consequence' of Sir Walter, Elizabeth and Mary. When Sir Walter asks for advice she tries to persuade him that his true interest lies in understanding that he should value honesty and not pride. Her arguments cannot penetrate Sir Walter's self-esteem, but in the case of Anne and Captain Wentworth a combination of possessive caution and prejudice has its effect. Lady Russell is sincere, cultivated and reasonable, and it is her integrity and love that give her persuasion its force. She does her best to love all the family, and in Anne's case there is no difficulty. The character of Lady Elliot is inscribed on the personality of this daughter at least. Over the matter of Sir Walter's debt, Lady Russell is the only one to think of consulting Anne, and of being influenced by her 'to a degree'. Sorrowful and angry at Elizabeth's disregarding of Anne in favour of Mrs Clay, Lady Russell would have rejoiced to see Anne marry Charles Musgrove, not because he was worthy of her, but because she would at least have been removed from what Lady Russell knows to be the 'partialities and injuries' of the Kellynch household.

On the two occasions when Lady Russell exercises what Anne regards as the rights and obligations of a mother, her judgement is mistaken and her persuasion is dangerous and destructive. Her formal assessment is conventional, untempered by individual sensitivity. Lady Russell's feelings about Anne's proposed engagement to Captain Wentworth, eight years previous to the main action of the novel, are reported (Ch.4,p.41 para. 3) in a manner suggesting the volatility of Lady Russell's thoughts at the time: 'to throw herself away . . . a young man . . . nothing but himself to recommend him . . . a most uncertain profession . . . a stranger without alliance or fortune'. The compressed, breathless style evokes Lady Russell's agitation at the prospect of change, and the possibility of a 'most wearing, anxious, youth-killing dependence'. The latter condition was only a possibility, as the narrative makes clear. It was pride, albeit of an infinitely less self-absorbed kind than Sir Walter's, that had determined Lady Russell's course of action. At the time the novel opens, when Anne is twenty-seven, she knows that Lady Russell had been wrong in giving such advice (Ch.4, p.43, para 1) because it meant the certainty of exchanging present happiness for indefinite misery on grounds which claimed to be absolute, but which could only be ratified by time (see Ch.23, p.212). Lady Russell's over-anxious caution had been unfortunate, an unnatural repression of youthful optimism and ardour, none the less disastrous for being well-meant. Lady Russell does not question the past, and when Anne has to speak of Captain Wentworth's return and the accident at Lyme, Lady Russell appears unmoved – the necessity of visiting Mrs Croft being a 'trial' to them both only in the sense that they must witness the possession of Kellynch by strangers. Internally, however, (in a rare shift of narrative stance from what is known to Anne, Ch.13, p.116) there is the ambivalence of unconscious doubt.

The Mr Elliot that Lady Russell meets at Bath is a gentleman, a man of substance, flawless in uniting wordly standing and sophistication with 'correct opinions and sensibilities'. The self-approving, emphatic tone in which her views are reported suggests the complacency with which she manages to reconcile improbabilities. Archly disclaiming deliberation, Lady Russell offers her opinion on the probability of Mr Elliot asking Anne to be his wife. In remembrance of Lady Elliot the recommendation becomes momentarily persuasive.

Lady Russell's character is more complicated than is sometimes allowed. In her fondness for Bath, window-curtains and the latest publications, she can override Anne's dislike of the town, and persuade herself that her god-daughter's feelings are the mistaken remnants of childhood associations, and that Anne's spirits will be improved by change and society. On hearing that Mr Elliot is in Bath, Lady Russell, who had lately spoken of herself as steady and matter-of-fact, recalls her pronouncement that Mr Elliot is a man in permanent disfavour, and she finds herself 'in a state of very agreeable curiosity and perplexity'. Lady Russell is simply less gifted than Anne in understanding people, and age and experience give her no advantage. Her mistakes are redeemed by her love for Anne, which is stronger than her vanity and her allegiance to convention, and her energies quickly adapt themselves to 'a new set of opinions and hopes'.

Elizabeth Elliot

'cold and unconcerned'

Vain, cold, snobbish, mercenary and unwise, Elizabeth's character is the antithesis of Anne's. Her self-centred frigidity rather invites silence than reproach, and Anne's few attempts to enlighten her are foiled by obstinacy. Elizabeth's capacity for self-deception is paralleled only by that of her father and Mary, but without having the extravagance that somehow alleviates condemnation. The treatment of Elizabeth is pitiless. In the cases of Lady Russell and Captain Wentworth, errors of judgement, once perceived, are forgiven; but Elizabeth has no affection to bestow, and no sense of responsibility or duty which might command respect. She is created to deserve her fate.

Sir Walter approves Elizabeth's beauty, and her admiration for rank complements his. At twenty-nine, with little charm or bloom lost, she is expected to marry 'suitably'. Only the inexplicably evasive conduct of Mr Elliot seems to have prevented the ideal union of the baronet's first daughter, for thirteen years the self-possessed mistress of Kellynch, with the presumed heir to the estate. Lacking this felicity, Elizabeth has to make do with her social standing in a scanty neighbourhood. She is perilously close to reaching an unmarriageable age, the years in which beauty must fade, to be followed by the final evil of inconsequence. The circle of Kellynch is as closed for Elizabeth as it seems to be for Anne. Polish is no compensation for uneventful residence without 'habits of utility . . . talents or accomplishments', and it is to this sameness that Elizabeth is returned after the unproductive glitter of Bath. Elizabeth appreciates Bath. With all the state commanded by a couple of servants, mistress of several rooms, cousin to the undistinguished Lady Dalrymple and the unfortunate Miss Carteret, friend of the freckled and scheming Mrs Clay, Elizabeth is as ridiculous as Mary, but her unredeeming blindness makes her a figure of oppression, and by her unnatural calculation she earns the disdain and contempt in which the reader, like Captain Wentworth, is forced to hold her.

Mary Musgrove

'Inheriting a considerable share of the Elliot self-importance'

A source of continual amusement to the reader, characterized by her speech, direct and reported, and by her letter, Mary is wilful, inconsistent and foolish. Self-important and self-pitying, without 'resources for solitude' or personal charm, Mary does little to recommend herself. 'Better endowed than the elder sister', nevertheless 'any indisposition sunk her completely'. Lying on the sofa that four summers and two children have faded, Mary complains of her health, Anne's tardiness, Lady Russell's neglect, Charles's absence, her unmanageable children and the Musgroves' noisy ignorance of what is due to an Elliot. It takes Anne's 'perseverance in patience' and 'forced cheerfulness' to divert Mary from the misery and affliction she invents.

Mary's ailments lessen with company, and her insensitivity may be freely exercised then. Anne, who has 'not a mother's feelings' must remain with the sick child, so that Mary can accompany the 'unfeeling' Charles to the Musgroves' to meet Captain Wentworth, and report blandly back to Anne that she is so altered that Frederick would not have known her again. Any attempt to evade the embarrassment of Mary's presence fails: she is 'very fond of a long walk' when the Musgrove girls desperately try to leave her behind, and vehement that, despite her virtuous impracticality, it is she who should be at Lyme with Louisa.

'Jealous and ill-judging' claims are typical of Mary. Captain

Benwick, whom Charles supposes to be interested in Anne, is 'rather my acquaintance', if a poor substitute for a real gentleman, who would be more attentive to falling scissors and a lady's commands than he would to the books that the dull Captain pores over. Mary considers that the Harvilles neglect their children when, in Louisa's interest, they send them to Uppercross; she, manifestly bored and irritated by hers, had become hysterical at her husband's proposal that she should return home.

Her vulgar enthusiasm for rank is another instance of Jane Austen's effective satire. Disposed to quarrel with the Musgroves over precedence, she scornfully advertises her shame at any connection with the Hayters. Ecstatic over the possibility of a chance meeting with her father's heir, it is only to be expected that Mary is delighted with the 'business' of Bath, and its opportunities for being introduced to people who matter. The best that can be said of Mary is that she means no ill. She is mildly 'gratified' by Anne's marriage because it reflects creditably upon herself, although it does promote Anne to seniority and a pretty carriage. Ironically, having decried the conversation of the Musgroves, their connections, their management of servants and even their sheer bulk, Mary's marriage to the future head of this family and the future proprietor of a landed estate becomes a powerful consolation – providing Captain Wentworth can be kept from being made a baronet.

Henrietta and Louisa Musgrove

'Henrietta was perhaps the prettiest, Louisa had the higher spirits'

Introduced at the end of Chapter 5, Louisa and Henrietta have 'all the usual stock of accomplishments' as if they have been trained to perform socially admirable tricks which are really only a gloss on their prettiness, even temperaments and happy upbringing by loving parents. Note the comparison of their mere enjoyments with Anne's superiority of mind and taste; her intellectual and cultural advantages cannot make up for the absence in Anne's life of the easy, natural affection the sisters have for one another.

They are young and pretty, with all the assurance of thousands of other young ladies, and it is no wonder that Admiral Croft hardly knows one from the other. When the sisters appear at Uppercross to comfort their sick nephew, their effervescent delight in Captain Wentworth is conveyed in compressed reported speech that captures their gushing rapidity and gleeful thoughtlessness of utterance. Their infatuation with Captain Wentworth is predictable, as is his distraction by them. Henrietta's head is turned only temporarily, and Charles Hayter's apparent reluctance to compete assures him of victory. Louisa is the elder sister, and completely unattached; on the walk to Winthrop by the accident of impulse and not deliberate art, she acts and speaks in a manner that moves and impresses Captain Wentworth. He 'honours' Louisa's enthusiasm for careering through life with the man she loves, and the conversation in the hedgerow, with Captain Wentworth's references to what he sees as 'firmness', appears to confirm that they are marked out for one another. Events at Lyme intend otherwise and, the well-meaning, shallow Louisa, convalescing in the company of the affectionate Captain Benwick, acquires a lifelong devotion to romantic literature as well as the navy. Speaking to Anne of the engagement, Captain Wentworth expresses his regard for Louisa as 'a very amiable, sweet-tempered girl, and not deficient in understanding', and admits to surprise that an intelligent, sensitive man like Benwick could so easily console himself.

Innocent and personable, but fundamentally ill-suited to be Frederick's wife, Louisa might well have been chosen, foolishly, by the young man – confident, rich, ready to fall in love and marry.

Mrs Clay

'a clever, insinuating, handsome woman, poor and plausible'

Mrs Clay's intention is to become Lady Elliot. She is handicapped by freckles and a projecting tooth, but her youth, intelligence and cleverly pleasing manner easily flatter Elizabeth and her father into insisting on her companionship. Lady Russell is severely provoked by Elizabeth's preference for this 'unequal' woman of 'dangerous' character. Anne is alert to the vulnerability of Sir Walter, and the doubtful future for Elizabeth should Sir Walter marry. Mr Elliot comes to Bath precisely because he has heard, from Colonel Wallis, of the possibility of Mrs Clay's succeeding in her intention. The occasional oblique references to the mutually antipathetic intrigues of Mr Elliot and Mrs Clay, and the eventual ironic concurrence of these in the departure for London, are cleverly constructed and entertaining; but neither Mrs Clay's character nor her part in the plot are developed.

Mrs Smith

'good sense and agreeable manners'

The introduction of Mrs Smith in Chapter 17 is to widen a perspective limited in the main to Anne's knowledge of events. The significance of Anne's friendship for this old acquaintance can be seen in several respects: Anne prefers the company of this self-reliant, impoverished widow to that of the illustrious Dalrymples; Mrs Smith's grim existence is a stark contrast to the decorative inanity of formal society; Anne learns about Mr Elliott's character.

Mrs Smith's kindness to Anne during the miserable period after the death of her mother would have been enough to command renewal of acquaintance, and her present suffering is an additional claim. There is no self-conscious comparison between the personal isolation Anne generally feels, and the desperate condition of her friend's existence, but we are told that Anne could scarcely envisage a situation more calculated to enfeeble the spirit. By her own tentative admission, Mrs Smith had failed to think seriously until it was too late, and now she has lost her husband, has no children to cherish, no family to support or comfort her in considerably reduced circumstances, and her health too poor to withstand misfortune. Mrs Smith has something more remarkable than determination or perseverance, 'the choicest gift of Heaven': 'that elasticity of mind, that disposition to be comforted, that power of turning readily from evil to good, and of finding employment which carried her out of herself, which was from Nature alone'. This stoicism is not a sentimental creation; Mrs Smith accepts the world's casual indifference phlegmatically, but not without sorrow for the weakness of human nature.

Dependent on the 'shrewd, intelligent, sensible' Nurse Rooke for her occupation and verbal contact with the world beyond the sick-room, Mrs Smith learns at fourth-hand that Anne may marry Mr Elliot. Her silence on the subject of the past, until she discovers that her supposition is mistaken, is explained rationally, but, because Mrs Smith's role is something of an arrangement, this is not convincing. The tale that she eventually tells (Ch.21) begins with Mrs Smith's own history, the dissipation of her youth, and of her personal knowledge of Mr Elliot's eagerness to auction any inheritance and the manner in which he made his fortune. A guiding principle of self-interest does not admit of exceptions, and Mrs Smith's requests that Mr Elliot, executor of her husband's will, should act on her behalf, were ignored. Bitterly resentful of this, and having discovered that Anne will never marry Mr Elliot, Mrs Smith, in making these disclosures, condemns him. They clarify the obscurity of Mr Elliot's pretence, making no difference, however, to Anne's intentions, and in the closing paragraphs the scheme of the novel rewards Mrs Smith for what she represents rather than for the effect of what she does.

Mr Elliot

'Mr Elliot was rational, discreet, polished, – but he was not open'

As the heir presumptive, Mr Elliot is referred to in the opening chapter, he appears enigmatically at Lyme, and at Bath he returns to the bosom of the family to mortify everyone apart from Anne. He is in personal contrast to Captain Wentworth, and is a source of some mystery and suspense; more is reported of him than he reveals for himself.

By the terms under which Sir Walter Elliot inherited the estate, in the event of his having no male child the estate is entailed upon the nearest male relation, who is William Walter Elliot, Esq. It is this 'heir presumptive' whom, we are told, Sir Walter courted assiduously, and whom Elizabeth admired mainly for his connection with her father (some years before the main action of the novel begins). However, a young law student at the time, he 'had purchased independence by uniting himself to a rich woman of inferior birth'. Worse still, and unpardonable to the Elliots, they were informed that he had spoken disrespectfully of the family and of his connection with it – affecting to despise the nobility, the 'honours' which would ultimately be his. At the beginning of the novel this 'awkward' history is concluded with an unstressed reference to the fact that Mr Elliot is now a widower.

In Chapter 12 Mr Elliot is re-introduced, in person this time, as the 'gentleman' who looks at Anne with that 'degree of earnest admiration' that has some effect on Captain Wentworth. Particularly as he is ignorant of Anne's identity, her cousin's general manner, considerate and polished, is a strong recommendation. At Bath Anne finds the shadowy Mr Elliot of the past transformed into an unfortunate victim of 'misapprehension', who is now not merely pardoned, but wholly and enthusiastically approved for 'great openness of conduct, such readiness to apologize for the past, such solicitude to be received as a relation again'. Anne's distrust of this reconstruction of character is rational but slight: 'the sensation of there being more than immediately appeared'. The reader may suspect, as does Anne, that the reason behind Mr Elliot's behaviour is his now being free, and inclined to pay his addresses to her sister. However, Lady Russell's veiled emphasis that time will tell is not lost on Anne either. She is therefore less surprised by his elaborate hint that he wishes her name might never change, than by his claim that he has long known of her. Mr Elliot's importance is in his being apparently presented as an alternative future for the heroine. Lady Russell's judgement on this point is clear. Mr Elliot unites personal virtues and family attachment, and Anne has once again to contend with persuasion. Mrs Smith's revelation of herself as the source of Mr Elliot's knowledge of Anne's character, and her eventual establishment of the truth about him follows Anne's decision, and confirms rather than inspires it. Anne endures the misery of seeing Mr Elliot assumed by Captain Wentworth to be a welcome suitor, before she knows from her friend that her cousin is 'a man without heart or conscience', who married for money, behaved with cruel irresponsibility to his friends and despised his family. His reported sincerity with regard to Anne and the baronetcy does not moderate her summary of his character: 'evidently a disingenuous, artificial, worldly man, who had never had any better principle to guide him than selfishness.' The logical conclusion of his machinations to keep Sir Walter single is for him to divert Mrs Clay himself, the implication being that his relentless pursuit of 'consequence' will be self-defeating.

Admiral and Mrs Croft

'His goodness of heart and simplicity of character were irresistible'
'Mrs Croft always met her (Anne) with a kindness which gave her the pleasure of fancying herself a favourite.'

The Crofts' renting of Kellynch brings Captain Wentworth as well as all the freshness and bluster of the sea to the claustrophobic narrowness of Anne's life. Admiral Croft is an engaging portrait of an officer devoted to the service, and quite unaffected by the wealth and rank it has brought him. Kellynch seems to offer no more than any other snug lodging, once the mirrors have been edged out of the way. He never alters his habits, walking always with his wife in Bath as in the country, just as she had invariably accompanied him to sea. To Anne the pair present 'a most attractive picture of happiness'. Characterized by his distinctive speech, the Admiral is honest, vigorous and unselfconscious.

A steady, sensible woman, evidently brave and resourceful, Mrs Croft scorns 'idle refinement'. Her 'keener powers' of observation make her a less generous admirer of the Musgrove sisters than her husband. With Mrs Harville, she sees Louisa's fall as 'the consequence of much thoughtlessness, and much imprudence'. Her shrewd comments (Ch.23) to Mrs Musgrove, on the inadvisability of a long engagement are overheard by Anne and Captain Wentworth. She enjoys naval company as much as the Admiral does, her knowledge and experience making her as 'intelligent and keen' as any of the men around her.

Mr and Mrs Musgrove

'friendly and hospitable, not much educated and not at all elegant'

According to their daughter-in-law, Mary, the Musgroves lack an understanding of, and a proper respect for, social distinction. Solid, respectable landowners, with all the domestic virtues and country interests, the senior Musgroves are 'in the old English style', which their children are attempting to modify, in forms gently satirized by the author.

The appearance of Captain Wentworth, an officer under whom her son briefly served, sends Mrs Musgrove into belated mourning for the 'stupid and unmanageable' Dick. Her 'large fat sighings' are, at the time, sincere; the description, sometimes regarded as cruel, is derisively intolerant of the inconsistency of a natural if absurd attempt by a mother of a large family to console herself for the loss of a child 'little cared for at any time by his family, though quite as much as he deserved; seldom heard of, and scarcely at all regretted.' Like the Musgroves' enthusiasm for guarding and destroying their game, the triviality of house-keeping and neighbourly business, and the 'quiet cheerfulness' of a cacophonous family Christmas, their style of life is often a matter for amusement, but, more importantly, it is presented as well-intentioned and basically successful. The parents love their children and are respected by them. Anne, whose worth is known by all of the family, comments on their response to the good luck of Henrietta and Louisa: 'Such excellent parents as Mr and Mrs Musgrove . . . should be happy in their children's marriages. They do everything to confer happiness I am sure. What a blessing to young people to be in such hands! Your father and mother seem so totally free from all those ambitious feelings which have led to so much misconduct and misery, both to young and old'. At Bath, Mrs Musgrove shows that her 'real affection' has been strengthened by Anne's usefulness, and her timely intervention in the family dispute over the play versus the party fortuitously gives Anne the opportunity of making a decisive declaration. The heartiness, warmth and sincerity of the Musgrove family are delightful to Anne, who has suffered the 'sad want of such blessings'.

Mr Shepherd

'a civil cautious lawyer'

Practical, and very much aware of his own interest and of the most appropriate means of obtaining it, Mr Shepherd uses Lady Russell's intercession to urge restraint on Sir Walter. Obsequious, plain 'John', he astutely manipulates Sir Walter into consideration of a naval officer as tenant of Kellynch Hall. He opens the conversation as if the newspaper has inspired him with a solution to their difficulties. Laughing dutifully at Sir Walter's laboured wit, Mr Shepherd flatters his employer into imagining that news of the availability of Kellynch Hall for rent will get about inevitably because of universal interest in Sir Walter. Eloquent in assuring Sir Walter that Admiral Croft is 'quite the gentlemen', and 'not likely to make the smallest difficulty about terms', Mr Shepherd makes it appear that the prospective tenant desires nothing more from the business than an association with a baronet.

Mr Shepherd does nothing more Machiavellian than drive

Mrs Clay over to Kellynch, and coyly use the word 'jealous' in recommending his own meticulous attention to Sir Walter's interests. Nevertheless, his character is a caustic sketch of a professional man, a parasite upon a feckless, unproductive landowner.

Captain Harville

'a perfect gentleman, unaffected, warm and obliging'

A minor character, Captain Harville has an important role in the development of the plot. A letter from him brings Captain Wentworth and his companions to Lyme. Captain Benwick is staying with the Harvilles when he meets Anne, and then sees so much of Louisa. After the Harvilles observe the apparent attachment between himself and Louisa, Captain Wentworth discovers that they consider him an engaged man. This timely and unintended warning sends Frederick on an extended visit to his married brother Edward. It is Captain Harville's wanting to be in Bath on business that suggests to Charles, Mary inevitably, and finally Mrs Musgrove and Henrietta, the suitability of a general excursion. Captain Wentworth is writing the letter concerning the miniature portrait on Captain Harville's behalf, when he overhears and reacts to the conversation between the latter and Anne.

Captain Harville and his wife live modestly, and their selfless devotion to their friends has 'bewitching charm'. Captain Harville's 'unaffected, easy kindness of manner' distinguishes his conversations with Anne – telling the story of Fanny Harville and Captain Benwick, of Captain Wentworth's support of his desolate friend, and in the long and moving debate in Chapter 23. Not one of the rich naval officers Mr Shepherd anticipates profiting from, and in poor health from a serious wound received two years earlier, Captain Harville is deeply attached to his family, his friends and, as his home and the flavour of his conversation illustrates, his profession, to the praise of which the author devotes the last words of the novel.

Captain Benwick

'He had an affectionate heart. He must love somebody'

'Uniting very strong feelings with quiet, serious and retiring manners', and having 'a decided taste for reading, and sedentary pursuits', Captain Benwick's mind is obviously one to appreciate that of Anne Elliot. Charles Musgrove tolerates Captain Benwick's head being full of books, and his having a taste for churches and such things because 'he has fought as well as read', and Charles's belief that Captain Benwick's behaviour at Lyme and his praise of Anne's 'elegance, sweetness, beauty' is an indication of a more permanent attachment is possibly shared by the reader. Captain Wentworth is surprised that this 'clever man, a reading man', can engage himself to Louisa after intense devotion to Fanny Harville, and Benwick's friend, Captain Harville, says, in sorrow not in anger, that 'she would not have forgotten him so soon'. Anne's awareness of Captain Benwick's willingness to excite strong feelings, that she feels one should taste but sparingly, leads her to recommend to him writing of the 'the highest precepts and strongest examples of moral and religious endurances'. His sincere but easy transference of affection comes as a surprise, and conveniently saves Captain Wentworth from the possibility of having 'in honour' to marry Louisa.

Sir Walter Elliot

'Vanity was the beginning and the end of Sir Walter's character'

Sir Walter's vanity of person and of situation is outrageous. The author's satirical presentation is a savage indictment of snobbery. Wholly self-regarding, a negligent parent, and an incompetent manager of his estates, Sir Walter is a decadent figure whose vulger ostentation is the reverse of refinement, and whose idea of a gentleman is that of a man of property or a well-sounding name.

Convinced that age withers everyone but himself, it is for pleasure and not reassurance that he fills Kellynch with mirrors, and to him appearance is an interest and a criterion second only to rank. He objects to the navy on both of these grounds. Although he acknowledges a 'utility' which he does not define, he complains of the tendency of the profession to promote men beyond their station and to age them prematurely. The staggering insensitivity of his comments is comic, and these are not confined to the navy: it is his belief that the multitude of ugly women in Bath are astounded by the appearance of someone like himself in company with the regrettably sandy-haired

Colonel Wallis; Mrs Clay's freckles have been quite carried away; Mary's nose is affected by sharp winds; decrepit Admiral Croft is known in Bath as the tenant of Kellynch Hall.

The parading of family connection with the Dalrymples is demeaning. Sir Walter has no conception of pride in the sense of self-respect, and the gradation of society he reveres is seen to be inconsistent with worth. Judging purely by appearance and by reference to position, he is incapable of acquiring the wisdom of experience; the natural prey of social predators like Mrs Clay and Mr Elliot, he learns nothing and is oblivious of his folly. The final chapter gives a corrosive account of him preparing his pen for application to the book of books, to record what he had considered, eight years previously, a degrading alliance, between his daughter (for whom he had no affection) and a penniless nobody: 'Captain Wentworth, with five-and-twenty thousand pounds, and as high in his profession as merit and activity could place him, was no longer nobody. He was now esteemed quite worthy to address the daughter of a foolish, spendthrift baronet, who had not principle or sense enough to maintain himself in the situation in which Providence had placed him.'

Charles Musgrove

'of good character and appearance'

The eldest son of a man of property and importance in the district second only to Sir Walter, Charles had had the good sense to ask Anne to marry him, and was then sufficiently good-tempered to withstand Mary's whims to the extent that 'they might pass for a happy couple'. He manages their children as well as his wife's interference will let him. Agreeing with his wife at least over their general shortage of funds, and the desirability of a generous gift from his parents, he defends his father's right to do as he pleases with his own money. He refuses to leave Lyme while Louisa's condition is uncertain, and hears with pleasure the news of Henrietta's engagement. His forthright, businesslike analysis of Charles Hayter's prospects shows that these are of considerably less importance to him than the fact that the man has been a lifelong friend. Trifling away his time zealously, preferring rat-hunting to books, Charles is amiable and boyish. His lack of 'powers of conversation or grace' ensure that the past is no threat. Anne admires him for his indefatigable good spirits, his kindness and lack of pretension, and is indebted to him for, among other things, his unequivocal enjoyment and his robust statement of his preference for a play over a private party of Dalrymples and Elliots, and, at the critical moment of their meeting Captain Wentworth, not scrupling to desert her for an appointment with a gunsmith.

Settings

Jane Austen's interest in character makes a detailed, realistic setting unnecessary. The breadth of contemporary society and culture do not concern the author. An impression only is given of upper-middle-class life in 1814. This impression is natural enough, but it is a selective representation. It refers to the country life of families who inherit the land, to the life of the families of naval officers, and to the social life to be found at a contemporary watering place, Bath.

When the story opens, we are shown what life was like in the country, at Kellynch Hall and at Uppercross. None of the men seems to have much to do; Sir Walter spends most of his time amusing himself, and his only reading is 'The Baronetage', which soothes his vanity. At Uppercross Mr Musgrove and his son 'had their own game to guard and to destroy, their own horses, dogs and newspapers to engage them'; in other words hunting, riding and shooting kept them tolerably busy at times. When Charles married, he did not leave his father's estate, but only moved to one of the farmhouses which had been converted into a cottage for him and his wife. Women were even more restricted in their activities, and had more time to spare than the men. They were always interested in 'housekeeping, neighbours, dress, dancing and music', Jane Austen tells us. Both men and women formed walking parties and spent autumn days strolling through the country lanes in groups. At night the families in the neighbourhood entertained each other to dinner and to impromptu parties, at which the daughters sang or played the piano or harp, and there was country dancing. Above all they talked, and many of their long, leisurely and sometimes tedious conversations are recorded for us. At Christmas time there were many happy family parties like that at Uppercross where, when Anne and Lady Russell called before setting out for Bath, we are told: 'On one side was a table occupied by some chattering girls, cutting up silk and gold paper; and on the other were tressels and trays, bending under the weight of brawn and cold pies, where riotous boys were holding high revel; the whole completed by a roaring Christmas fire, which seemed determined to be heard in spite of all noise of the others.' In days of few schools and slow transport the children were sent away to be educated at boarding schools; Louisa and Henrietta Musgrove had just returned from such a school at Exeter where they had acquired the 'stock accomplishments'; the younger children were still away. Anne was educated at a similar school, for it was there that she knew Mrs Smith, then Miss Hamilton. When they left school the girls did not train for careers, of course, but returned home to wait until they found husbands, and the position of the girl who did not marry was far from enviable. Women were always under the authority of some male relative, usually husband or father, unless they become widows, when they were allowed to have some control of their own affairs. Most families gave their daughters the benefit of a few weeks in London each spring to enjoy the pleasures of the world of fashion, but with the Elliot family it seems to have been only Elizabeth, the eldest daughter, who received this advantage.

The scenes at Lyme suggest the life of the naval officers and their wives who have left the sea either temporarily, like Captain Wentworth, or permanently, like Admiral Croft, and come to live among those who have travelled little. These are a race apart, intelligent, keen and very tender-hearted. Some officers' wives were accustomed to voyaging with their husbands and sharing the dangers of encounters with Napoleon's navy. Mrs Croft declares that the ships were very comfortable, especially the larger ones, and even in a frigate, although the travellers must of necessity be more confined, the accommodation was good. 'Any reasonable woman may be perfectly happy in one of them', she says. Captain Wentworth, on the other hand, hated to see women on board, and reminded his sister that she was travelling with her husband as captain.

Next to London with the ladies and gentlemen of quality came Bath, where people came to take the waters and to meet their friends. They travelled by carriage or curricle, and as it was usually in the winter that they made these migrations, the journeys must have been arduous. Life in Bath was much more varied than life in the country for both men and women. By day the men drank the waters and had their guns and other sporting equipment repaired, while the ladies went shopping to match ribbons or change their library books. At night there were many amusements – the theatre, concerts, dances, and gaiety for everyone. The conventions were strictly observed, with much homage paid to rank and wealth, order of precedence, formal calls and the leaving of cards. Ladies curtsied when they met friends. Dress was most important, but the novel gives us few details.

As Anne responds to the events which take place, the several locations of the novel have a particular importance, and in this respect separate discussion of aspects of the work should not preclude an understanding of overlapping and interrelation. Setting provides structure and illustrates theme.

Themes

The surface calm and order of *Persuasion* has a hypnotic charm which can deceive readers into accepting or rejecting the book as a drawing-room piece, a rather refined romantic novel. It is a love story, and a comedy, but the characterization, the structure and the prevailing ironic tone of the narrative, force the serious consideration of a number of ideas. Snobbery, pride, vanity, self-deception, hypocrisy and self-interest are examined in opposition to rectitude, understanding, sympathy and selflessness. The public world of occupation and convention, economic dependence and sufficiency, courtship leading to marriage encircles the essentially private experience of interpretation and judgement.

Persuasion amounts to a critique of society, though not in any didactic or theoretical sense. Standards are often applied by the imperfect, façades are obtrusive. The pseudo-aristocracy, infected by debilitating snobbery and liable to undermining by acquisitive pursuers of wealth and fame, are satirized mercilessly as useless, feckless and corrupt. The gentry are ironically observed, their uncultivated complacency tolerated. The naval officers, a professional class, are made distinctive characters, not ciphers, in a recognizably naturalistic mould. They are as genuinely admirable for 'their friendliness, their brotherliness, their uprightness' (as Louisa trills), as they are distinguished, in the sober final phrase of the novel, for their national importance. The health of the social organism depends upon both the re-affirmation of social values by honest, principled individual attestation, and by the responsible, disinterested activity of constituent groups.

The novel examines the moral nature of the individual, testing character and conduct against the background of values not called into question. The quality of a character's sensitivity and intelligence determines their capacity for evaluation. The recurrent problems facing the protagonist are the discrepancy between what the world is and what it ought to be, the difficulty of perceiving accurately, the necessity of choice and the understanding of and adherence to the principles that inform judgement. The search for truth is a painful self-realization, and strength of character is needed to withstand life's persuasions. Faithfulness and steadfastness in duty and in love are declared to deserve reward; and, in the ideal world of fiction, to receive it. There is conflict between values, between the prudent authority of Lady Russell, for example, and the passionate love of Anne for Captain Wentworth. This can only be resolved by a balancing of impulse by order. Anything less than fidelity to what is felt to be right would be a compromise that might lead to gratification, but never to happiness. A character's 'true interest' can be served only by doing what is 'correct': 'Lady Elliot had been an excellent woman, sensible and amiable; whose judgement and conduct, if they might be pardoned the youthful infatuation which made her Lady Elliot, had never required indulgence afterwards. She humoured, or softened, or concealed his failings, and promoted his real respectability for seventeen years; and though not the very happiest being in the world herself, had found enough in her duties, her friends, and her children, to attach her to life, and make it no matter of indifference to her when she was called on to quit them.'

Structure

The story is told for the most part as Anne experiences it. She is a fixed point from which other characters are seen, enacting their lives and giving their respective definitions of love, and towards whose constancy Frederick moves. Two episodes of major importance to the story are given in retrospect: the early love of Captain Wentworth and Anne Elliot, and Lady Russell's persuasion. The structure summarizes the past and elaborates the thoughts and feelings of the heroine as she relives those events, and tries to discern the meaning of the present.

Beginning with Anne's original circumstances at Kellynch, introducing Captain Wentworth at Uppercross, with crisis developing at Lyme and being resolved at Bath, the movement of the novel takes Anne from hesitation to confidence, and Frederick from pride and anger to understanding. Time had softened Anne's attachment to Captain Wentworth, but she was 'Too dependent on time alone; no aid had been given in change of place . . . or in any novelty or enlargement of society.' The Kellynch circle had not been broken. The emptiness of Anne's life is suggested by her silence, and the preoccupation of her family with evading the inevitable social embarrassments that follow the careless management of the estate. Uppercross is three miles away. There is warmth here, although little refinement. This change is an accentuation of her suffering, for it forces on her the illusion of a possibility which the facts seem to deny. Anne's observation of Louisa Musgrove and Captain Wentworth making fools of themselves is a solitary anguish. The charm of Lyme and the hospitality of Captain Wentworth's friends bring a freedom and indepedence of spirit that have an effect in themselves. At some time or other, chance will demonstrate the obvious, and the accident on the Cobb is the turning point of the story. Captain Wentworth's eyes are opened, although the restricted point of view of the narrative prevents us from knowing this. Suspense is maintained as the characters move to Bath, where the movement is ritual, a public parading of acquaintance and observance of convention, with private exchanges barely practicable even should chance permit them. Resolution or separation is made to depend upon natural events, and equally naturally, the reversal of the central characters' positions, with Captain Wentworth silently watching Anne and Mr Elliot, is not clearly delineated until Frederick gives his own account of what has happened.

There is representative use of setting, to group characters, and to provide appropriate background for the different sections of society in which Anne moves. The standards of Kellynch – those of titled gentry, who are weakened rather than elevated by regarding themselves as nobility – can be contrasted with those of an unambitious squirearchy and a meritocratic navy, each of which has a natural gentility. The whirligig of Bath is where the heroine must exercise her judgement.

It is impossible not to see things as Anne does. The reader rarely knows more. Devices like the letters and Mrs Smith's retrospect, which introduce material necessarily withheld and focus interest on Anne's response rather than the original event, mean that the narrative never leaves her, and the ironic narration is often an enlargement of her thought; it appeals (directly sometimes and more often by implication) to a view of society that is Anne's and is assumed to be that of the reader.

Other characters have a greater independence than they would have in a more openly subjective, first person account. The great scenes of the novel, dramatic dialogue such as that which takes place between Anne and Captain Wentworth when they finally resolve their differences, have an immediacy and an objectivity which they could not otherwise have. At the same time the occasional use of impressionistic, reported speech or thought gives a suggestion of the workings of a particular mind, open to the narrator and the reader but not necessarily to Anne.

Persuasion was published posthumously, and although the cancelled chapter shows that the novel had been radically revised, and we know that Jane Austen had described it as being ready for publication, had she not been seriously ill when completing it, she might have revised it further. Certain important characters, Lady Russell and Mr Elliot for example, are relatively undeveloped; and the reader may be uneasy about the introduction of Mrs Smith, and particularly in the matter of her withholding of information.

Style

Typically, the prose is formal and elegant. Sentences are often complex, symmetrical structures, precisely informative, non-figurative and unambiguous:

There could not be an objection. There could only be a most proper alacrity, a most obliging compliance for public view; and smiles reined in and spirits dancing in private rapture. In half a minute, Charles was at the bottom of Union-street again, and the other two proceeding together; and soon words enough had passed between them to decide their direction towards the comparatively quiet and retired gravel-walk, where the power of conversation would make the present hour a blessing indeed; and prepare for it all the immortality which the happiest recollections of their own future lives could bestow.

Variation in sentence length gives an infusion of emotion through rhythm and pace: 'They had no conversation together, no intercourse but what the commonest civility required. Once so much to each other! Now nothing! There *had* been a time, when of all the large party now filling the drawing-room at Uppercross, they would have found it most difficult to cease to speak to one another. With the exception, perhaps, of Admiral and Mrs Croft, who seemed particularly attached and happy, (Anne could allow no other exception even among the married couples) there could have been no two hearts so open, no tastes so similar, no feelings so in unison, no countenances so beloved. Now they were as strangers; nay, worse than strangers, for they could never become acquainted. It was a perpetual estrangement.'

The narrative voice is authoritative in tone. There is an objectivity and omniscience which gives an assurance the reader does not question:

Lady Russell was most anxiously zealous on the subject, and gave it much serious consideration. She was a woman rather of sound than quick abilities, whose difficulties in coming to any decision in this instance were great, from the opposition of two leading principles. She was of strict integrity herself, with a delicate sense of honour; but she was as desirous of saving Sir Walter's feelings, as solicitous for the credit of the family, as aristocratic in her ideas of what was due to them, as any body of sense and honesty could well be.

Epigrammatic generalizations appeal directly to the reader for confirmation of insight: 'How quick come the reasons for approving what we like!'; 'Husbands and wives generally understand when opposition will be in vain'; 'Personal size and mental sorrow have certainly no necessary proportions'. The guiding intelligence is cool, and emotion is always under control. Realism is preferred to sentimentality: 'Half the sum of attraction, on either side, might have been enough, for he had nothing to do, and she had hardly any body to love.' Formal description carries evocative suggestions: 'the remarkable situation of the town, the principal street almost hurrying into the water, the walk to the Cobb, skirting round the pleasant little bay, which in the season is animated with bathing machines and company, the Cobb itself, its old and new improvements, with the very beautiful line of cliffs stretching out to the east of the town, are what the stranger's eye will seek.' There is impressionistic illustration of the clutter of detail: 'She was now lying on the faded sofa of the pretty little drawing-room, the once elegant furniture of which had been gradually growing shabby, under the influence of four summers and two children.'

An important feature of Jane Austen's style is the assumption implied in the use of particular words. Reference is continually made to abstractions: character, prudence, authority, guidance, good principles and instruction, right-mindedness, justice and equity, duty. The premise is that the reader shares with the author a view of what is important in life, of what constitutes right in an ordered world: 'Lady Elliot had promoted the "real" respectability of Sir Walter', and Anne's character would have been valued by people of 'real' understanding; the 'true' dignity of Sir Walter would have been served by honesty and not by false pride.

Physical action in *Persuasion* has minimal importance. The fall on the Cobb is a device to prove a point. Jane Austen is less at ease with 'The horror of that moment to all who stood around!' than she is reporting the boatmen collecting 'to enjoy the sight of a dead young lady, nay two dead young ladies'. Characters do walk in and out of rooms, and get in and out of carriages, but what matters is what they think, say, and understand. The dramatic scenes of the novel are conversations. Speech is summarized, reported indirectly and directly, and thought is stated and implied in a flexible and subtle manner. Idiosyncratic speech fits perfectly in character: 'A new sort of way this, for a fellow to be making love, by breaking his mistress's head!' Sir Walter expounding his objections to the navy (Ch.3, p.36) is astringent satire. Like their father, Elizabeth and Mary reveal themselves by what they say: ' "I cannot possibly do without Anne," was Mary's reasoning; and Elizabeth's reply was, "Then I am sure Anne had better stay, for nobody will want her in Bath." ' The flow of a character's thought is sometimes suggested by a condensing of speech, the introductory reporting clause being omitted, accelerating time and giving an ironic detachment to the narrative: 'Lady Russell felt obliged to oppose her dear Anne's known wishes. It would be too much to expect Sir Walter to descend into a small house in his own neighbourhood. Anne herself would have found the modifications of it more than she foresaw, and to Sir Walter's feelings they must have been dreadful.' Free reporting has the immediacy of direct speech and the compression of indirect: 'the two young aunts were able so far to digress from their nephew's state, as to give the information of Captain Wentworth's visit; – staying five minutes behind their father and mother, to endeavour to express how perfectly delighted they were with him, how much handsomer, how infinitely more agreeable they thought him than any individual among their male acquaintance, who had been at all a favourite before – how glad they had been to hear papa invite him to dinner – how sorry when he said it was quite out of his power and how glad again, when he had promised in reply to papa and mamma's farther pressing invitations, to come and dine with them on the morrow, actually on the morrow!'

The distinguishing feature of Jane Austen's comic art is an infectious irony. It is a cast of mind, an acute awareness of incongruity, contradiction, paradox, and anomaly that gives the style a special resonance in which what is stated is invariably less than, in opposition to, or in some tension with, what is meant. It finds character and conduct perfectly complacent and ludicrously deficient by any criteria the author and the implied reader would call civilized. The understatement has a force of its own. The narrative shifts from the objective to the ironic mode when adopting a particular character's attitude to the material related: 'A few years before, Anne Elliot had been a very pretty girl, but her bloom had vanished early; and as even in its height, her father had found little to admire in her (so totally different were her delicate features and mild dark eyes from his own); there could be nothing in them now that she was faded and thin, to excite his esteem. He had never indulged much hope, he had now none, of ever reading her name in any other page of his favourite work.' In a story about depth and constancy of feeling, irony controls any lurch to excess: 'On the morning appointed for Admiral and Mrs Croft's seeing Kellynch Hall, Anne found it most natural to take her almost daily walk to Lady Russell's and keep out of the way till all was over; when she found it most natural to be sorry that she had missed the opportunity of seeing them.' Through its psychological realism it exposes a tendency to self-delusion: ' "Very well", said Elizabeth, "I have nothing to send but my love." ' It cannot be more cruel – or honest – than this, even in the celebrated instances of Mrs Musgrove's 'large fat sighings', and Mrs Clay's stopping to consider what she might do for a clergyman. A covert appeal, made to the reader's judgement, can be as persuasive as it is brief. Sir Walter prepares to show himself to his 'afflicted' tenants so that they may express regret; furniture imported by the Musgrove daughters gives a 'proper' air of confusion to the Great House; Captain Benwick has the melancholy air he 'ought' to have. The comedy is a shared response, distanced emotionally, but not intellectually or morally, from its subject matter.

General questions

1 What are the distinctive features of Jane Austen's characterization?

Guidelines for note-form answer

    a) General description/history, e.g. Sir Walter Elliot, Captain Wentworth. Select details and relevant brief quotations.

    b) Generalizations on conduct, e.g. Lady Russell. Quote and establish the views, attitudes etc. of Lady Russell.

    c) How characters are seen by others, e.g. Captain Wentworth by Anne. Detail the reactions of each and the constant awareness of the other. Quote.

    d) How they see themselves, e.g. Elizabeth and Mary (irony of narration). Speech of each, what it reveals (contrast with Anne).

    e) What conduct reveals, e.g. Mary, Louisa and Henrietta – refer particularly to the last two, how they appear to the reader etc.

    f) Speech that distinguishes, e.g. Charles Musgrove and Admiral Croft, and that which reveals, e.g. Sir Walter and Elizabeth.

    g) By the structure and style of the novel: Anne Elliot – since she is the central character, this must be the conclusion as well.

2 What impression of middle-class society in the eighteenth century does Jane Austen create in *Persuasion*?

3 Does *Persuasion* offer an insight into human nature in any age, or is it a study of individuals in a particular place at a particular time?

4 Do you agree that the scenes of domestic comedy are the most amusing and convincing?

5 'In *Persuasion* the story is embedded in a study of snobbery.' Discuss.

6 What differing conceptions of love are illustrated by the characters in *Persuasion*?

7 What are the key episodes leading to the reconciliation of Anne and Frederick?

8 Give an account of the part played in the novel by each of the following: Mrs Clay, Charles Hayter, Mr Shepherd, Nurse Rooke.

9 What parallels and contrasts in character or situation can you find in the novel?

10 Examine the significance of the family groupings in *Persuasion*.

11 How important are the settings in the story?

12 Do you find Anne either 'almost a tragically noble figure' or 'unnaturally virtuous and passive'?

13 Contrast Captain Wentworth with Mr Elliot.

14 Do you agree that there is a 'peculiar beauty and a peculiar dullness' in *Persuasion*?

15 'What calm lives they had, those people.' Is this a sound judgement of the world of *Persuasion*?

16 Do you agree that in Jane Austen's style in *Persuasion*, irony is pervasive?

17 Write a careful account of what you consider to be the main theme of *Persuasion* in relation to the title of the novel.

18 In what ways does *Persuasion* illustrate Jane Austen's talents as a comic novelist?

19 Discuss the varieties of folly presented in the novel.

20 Jane Austen presents a society in which almost everything appears to differ from our own. Why, nevertheless, does she hold the attention of the modern reader?

Further reading

Jane Austen, *Sense and Sensibility, Pride and Prejudice, Emma, Mansfield Park, Northanger Abbey*

Mary Lascelles, *Jane Austen and her Art* (O.U.P., 1939)

W. A. Craik, *Jane Austen, The Six Novels* (Methuen, 1965)

R. Liddell, *The Novels of Jane Austen* (London, 1963)

J. E. Austen-Leigh, *Memoir of Jane Austen* ed. R. W. Chapman (O.U.P.)

W.A. Craik, *Jane Austen in her Time* (Nelson, 1967)

C. Gillie, *A Preface to Jane Austen* (Longman, 1972)

Barbara Hardy, *A Reading of Jane Austen* (Athlone Press, 1979)

Pan study aids Selected titles published in the Brodie's Notes series

Jane Austen Emma Mansfield Park Northanger Abbey Persuasion
Pride and Prejudice

Geoffrey Chaucer (parallel texts editions) The Franklin's Tale
The Knight's Tale The Miller's Tale The Nun's Priest's Tale
The Pardoner's Tale Prologue to the Canterbury Tales
The Wife of Bath's Tale

Joseph Conrad The Nigger of the Narcissus & Youth
The Secret Agent

Charles Dickens Bleak House David Copperfield Dombey and Son
Great Expectations Hard Times Little Dorrit Oliver Twist
Our Mutual Friend A Tale of Two Cities

George Eliot Middlemarch The Mill on the Floss Silas Marner

E. M. Forster Howards End A Passage to India
Where Angels Fear to Tread

William Golding Lord of the Flies The Spire

Graham Greene Brighton Rock The Power and the Glory
The Quiet American

Thomas Hardy Chosen Poems of Thomas Hardy
Far from the Madding Crowd Jude the Obscure
The Mayor of Casterbridge Return of the Native
Tess of the d'Urbervilles The Trumpet-Major

L. P. Hartley The Go-Between The Shrimp and the Anemone

Laurie Lee As I Walked Out One Midsummer Morning
Cider with Rosie

Christopher Marlowe Doctor Faustus Edward the Second

John Milton A Choice of Milton's Verse Comus and Samson
Agonistes Paradise Lost I, II

Sean O'Casey Juno and the Paycock
The Shadow of a Gunman and the Plough and the Stars

George Orwell Animal Farm 1984

William Shakespeare Antony and Cleopatra As You Like It
Coriolanus Hamlet Henry IV (Part I) Henry IV (Part II) Henry V
Julius Caesar King Lear Love's Labour's Lost Macbeth Measure for
Measure The Merchant of Venice A Midsummer Night's Dream
Much Ado about Nothing Othello Richard II Richard III Romeo and
Juliet The Sonnets The Taming of the Shrew The Tempest Twelfth
Night The Winter's Tale

les personnes qui comprennent vraiment.
La préocupation des apparences personnelles et
et de la position sociale est rendu ridicule par
des comparaison déprécier avec la "reel"
sectabilité qui reconnait les qualités d'Anne
et les bonne disposition de sa mère.. Il y a un
appel à 1 notion de réalité inconnu de Sir
W. et d'Eli.. Anne, par contre, genereuse et
intelligente, est seule dans une famille dont
par ses mesure⁼, elle n'est rien. La mauvaise
quels "   .   posture d'Elizabeth
peut ê inenviable, mais le ton critique de
sur le cas de son égoïsme mercenaire la rend
impossible (ou incapable) de sympathiser avec ses
regrets et ses apprehensions ī elle approche les
"années de danger". A travers la concentrat⁼
sur [faux] miroir des Elliot, et la présentat⁼
(monde) d'Anne une majeur partie
de 1 ironique des considérat⁼ de Sir Walter ā
(feinte) son égards cō une " déteinte et
maigre " créature de valeur inférieure,
propre decept⁼ ou cō oppressive. L'incon-
cidérer de la positi⁼ d'Anne, est la dépendance
plus poignante pour ces amoindriss⁼ des faits

pendant l'été de 1814, sir Walther Elliot, baron
un veuf avec 1 fille marié, et 2 vivant avec
lui à Kellynch Hall, trouve que sa propriété
de famille ne fournit pas un revenu suffisant
pour couvrir les dépenses de son ménage

Commentaire

Les ennuis de Sir Walter proviennent de sa
propre affaire. Sans la direction digne de
confiance de Lady Elliot le baron vit en des
sous de ses resources, encouragé par son
aînée (fille) qui partage les idées de son père
en ce qui concerne le ce qu'on doit au rang
et à la beauté. la propriété est entraîné et ne
peut pas ê hypothèquée davantage. Sir Walter
n'ayant pas de fils, l'héritier présomptif est
William Walter Eliott avec qui Elizabeth
parle de se marier.
L'auteur indifferent, le ton de narration ironique
offert. un exposé absurde : terre à terre des
concidérat : de Sir Walter pr lui-m̄. Le "livre
des livres" est la seule littérature que le baron
choisisse de lire, et son intérêt est tjs dimulé
par l'entreé faite dans son propre nom.
Son histoire de famille est avec beauté reduit
à 2 in-douze pages du travail de ~~printps~~
l'imprimeur. Le narcissisme sans cervelle de
Sir Walter est établit avant (the formal),
terre à terre, ~~une~~ voie narrative omnisciente
qui détache son histoire et son caractère. Avec
le l'Imbroglio équilibré de prose qui donne un
merveilleux portrait du vide, le lecteur sent
l'extravagante vanité avant qu'elle ne soit
exposée; et il y a un contrat implicité
entre les valeurs des Elliot de Kellynch H et
celles parhasé: par l'auteur, ~~les~~ lecteurs et

chap. 2.

Mᵉ Shepherd, l'agent de Sir W., et lady Russel encouragé par Anne — conseillent des économie. sévère que Sir W. et Eli. ne peuvent pas approver. En effet, Kellynch Hall devra ê laissé et la famille vivra à Bath.

Commentary

Le chapitre est un model de persuasion; honnêteté, justice, respectabilité, prudence, un dignitée et échec principaux pour ~~faire~~ donner 1 impression sur ~~les~~ intérêts personnels et les sentiments d'1 gentleman. Mr Shepherd, finement entendu, et voya ~~vanitée~~ ses intérêts personnels, délaisse lady Russel, pour proposer une sorte d'actᵉ inévitable mᵃⁱˢ impopulaire. Il tire avantage du recul de Sir W., de la disgrace de vivre sans apparat pour proposer l'évacuatᵉ de Kellynch ~~te~~ pour Bath potentiellement moins chers.